C000129363

Good Housekeeping

GOOD FOOD IN
30 MINUTES

Good Housekeeping

GOOD FOOD IN
30 MINUTES

EBURY PRESS
LONDON

First published 1995

1 3 5 7 9 10 8 6 4 2

Text © Ebury Press and/or the National Magazine Company Ltd 1995

All rights reserved. No part of this publication may be reproduced, stored in a retrieval system, or transmitted in any form or by any means, electronic, mechanical, photocopying, recording or otherwise, without the prior permission of the copyright owners.

The expression GOOD HOUSEKEEPING as used in the title of the book is the trade mark of the National Magazine Company Limited and The Hearst Corporation, registered in the United Kingdom and USA, and other principal countries of the world, and is the absolute property of the National Magazine Company Limited and The Hearst Corporation. The use of this trade mark other than with the express permission of The National Magazine Company Limited or The Hearst Corporation is strictly prohibited.

First published in the United Kingdom in 1995 by Ebury Press
Random House, 20 Vauxhall Bridge Road, London SW1V 2SA

Random House Australia (Pty) Limited
20 Alfred Street, Milsons Point, Sydney, New South Wales 2061, Australia

Random House New Zealand Limited
18 Poland Road, Glenfield, Auckland 10, New Zealand

Random House South Africa (Pty) Limited
PO Box 337, Bergvlei, South Africa

Random House UK Limited Reg. No. 954009

A CIP catalogue record for this book is available from the British Library.

Edited by Helen Southall
Designed by Jerry Goldie

ISBN 0 09 180805 7

Typeset from disk by SX Composing, Essex
Printed and bound in England by Clays Ltd, St Ives plc

Papers used by Ebury Press are natural recyclable products made from wood grown in sustainable forests. In addition, the paper used in this book is recycled.

Contents

Introduction

In today's modern kitchen, and with a little organization, it is easily possible to rustle up a delicious meal in the time it takes to reheat a prepacked, ready-prepared meal. Access to good food shops and markets helps enormously – a gleaming fresh sole grills in no time and is hard to beat topped with a knob of herb butter; a grilled steak with a crisp green salad, fresh pasta or a risotto are all quick and uncomplicated to cook and make the best of good fresh ingredients. For the days when it's not possible to base a meal on fresh ingredients, a well stocked storecupboard, fridge and freezer are essential. Don't get stuck in a 'meat and two veg' pattern of eating. Think soup and crostini; prawn, vegetable and noodle stir-fry; salad and bread; lentil dal and rice; and, of course, pasta, pasta, pasta. What you keep in your kitchen cupboards is very much a matter of personal taste, but a few well chosen basics should mean that you can rustle up a hot, tasty meal in no time.

STORECUPBOARD BASICS

CANNED FOODS

Consommé Better than a stock cube in soups, risottos and pan-fried meat dishes.

Pulses For soups, dips, salads and quick stews. Rinse and drain beans thoroughly before using. Remember that they lose much of their bite during the canning process so add them towards the end of cooking. Use this to your advantage by puréeing them in a food processor to make quick dips. Try blending flageolet beans with fresh mint thinned with olive oil. Serve warm with grilled lamb. Or mash red kidney beans and fry with plenty of chilli and garlic and a splash of water. Top with grated cheese, grill until melted and serve with tortilla chips.

Tuna For fish cakes, salade niçoise and *tonno e fagioli* (can of tuna, can of cannellini beans, garlic dressing, sliced onion, parsley and grated lemon rind).

Anchovies Chop with garlic, chillies, capers and parsley, and toss with cooked pasta; mash with garlic and rosemary and spread on lamb before grilling; toss with salad leaves and garlic croûtons; purée with garlic, basil, olive oil, tomato purée and red wine vinegar to make *anchoiade* for spreading on toasted ciabatta.

Coconut milk For instant curries, soups and sauces.

Chopped tomatoes For innumerable sauces as well as stews and soups.

DRIED FOODS

Rice Arborio for risotto; basmati for pilau.

Pasta Spaghetti for tossing with pesto, with chilli and oil, or with butter and Parmesan; penne or conchiglie for tomato sauces; and swift-cooking angel-hair pasta for when time is really short.

Split red lentils They don't need soaking and they cook quickly. Use in curries and dal, and for thickening soups.

Dried mushrooms Porcini or cep for risotto, bruschetta, pasta and a richly flavoured sauce for poultry or meat; shiitake for stir-fries.

Dried chillies To perk up all manner of things.

Saffron Adds luxurious subtlety to risotto, creamy sauces and potato salads.

Dried spices Keep a good selection, if you have the space, including whole nutmegs, coriander seeds, cumin, cinnamon sticks, paprika and black peppercorns.

Biscotti (cantuccini) With mascarpone for dessert, or for munching with coffee.

Dried apricots For nibbling straight from the packet, or for duck and rice dishes.

BOTTLES AND JARS

Capers For their welcome piquancy in salads and fishy things.

Sweet peppers For speedy salsas, salads and pizzas. Purée in a blender and thin with oil or something creamy (see below) to make a sauce for pasta, meat or fish, or a dip for pitta bread and crudités.

Sun-dried tomatoes For pasta, salads, tomato sauces, vegetables, bruschetta.

Artichoke hearts For omelettes, salads, bruschetta, pizza and antipasto.

Tapenade or olive paste For bruschetta and grilled meats, or thin with cream and toss with pasta.

Pesto For pasta, of course, but also for flavouring dressings, soups, sauces and grilled or steamed vegetables.

Peanut butter For satay sauce and Indonesian-style salad dressings.

Oils Extra-virgin olive oil for drizzling on pasta, salads and vegetables, as well as a cheaper, plainer olive oil and a bland vegetable oil for frying.

Vinegars Balsamic is perfect for sprinkling sparingly on salad leaves and vegetables. Wine vinegars are useful for dressings, and for deglazing after frying.

Mustards and pickles To pep up leftover meats and transform plain sandwiches.

Curry paste Frowned on by serious cooks, but it tastes better than curry powder. Since the spices have already been cooked it can be used straight from the jar.

Tomato ketchup For bacon sandwiches, as well as for barbecue sauce (4 parts ketchup, 1 part mustard, 1 part honey, 1 part Worcestershire sauce).

F R I D G E   F A R E

Parmesan cheese Grate on to pasta or make shavings with a potato peeler and scatter over salads and vegetables. Toss together with fresh rocket, juicy pears, a little parma ham, freshly ground pepper, coarse sea salt and virgin olive oil.

Olives in oil Preferably from a delicatessen, these are perfect for staving off hunger while you cook, and for salads, pizza and pasta.

Hummus For baked potatoes, dressings, pasta or with olives, hot pitta bread, chunks of cucumber and yogurt for a quick Greek *mezze*-style meal.

Good tasty butter For hot bread, omelettes and vegetables, or melted with hot pasta and freshly grated Parmesan.

Large free-range eggs For omelettes, pancakes, tortilla and all the classics – boiled, scrambled, poached or fried. Or for *zabaglioni* (see page 218).

Salami or ham For bruschetta, antipasto, salads and pizzas.

Goat's cheese For grilling or baking on toast. Stuff it under the skin of chicken breast fillets, or try it diced and tossed with hot pasta and herbs.

Mozzarella cheese For tomato, basil, mozzarella and avocado salad; for improving shop-bought pizzas; and for *mozzarella in carozza* (mozzarella sandwiches, coated in beaten egg, then seasoned flour, then more egg, and shallow-fried for about 3 minutes on each side until golden). Serve hot with chutney and salad.

Peppered mackerel fillets Vacuum-packed fish keeps well. Use it in salads – it's particularly good with canned beans. Puréed with cream cheese it makes pâté or a topping for baked potatoes.

Lemons Juice adds a lively edge to anything grilled – fish, obviously, but try it with lamb. Grated rind adds verve to rice, steamed vegetables, bean salads and garlic butter.

Mayonnaise Straight from the jar for BLTs, or flavoured with garlic, lemon or herbs with baked potatoes, fish, salads and chips.

Something creamy For enriching meat and pasta sauces and dressings. This could be cream (single or double, or even one of the reduced-calorie cream substitutes), crème fraîche, mascarpone or cream cheese or yogurt.

Pancetta or bacon For its irresistible flavour and smell. Cook until crisp, and crumble on to salads or baked potatoes, or mix with breadcrumbs and Parmesan and use to stuff large mushrooms, drizzle with oil and bake for 15 minutes.

VEGETABLE RACK

Garlic You either love it or hate it. Indispensable if you love it.

Onions, potatoes and carrots Because they keep well and they're so versatile.

FREEZER

Bread Freeze part-baked baguettes or ciabatta as well as fully baked loaves and pitta breads. Warm bread from the oven can form the centrepiece of numerous fast suppers. Try it with unsalted butter, a ripe, runny camembert and some olives. A hastily made salad is better with warm bread, and fresh bread will transform the most mundane sandwich.

Pasta Fresh pasta cooks from frozen in less time than dried pasta. Stuffed ravioli or tortellini freeze well (brands without meat are best). Serve with butter and grated Parmesan or bottled pesto.

Frozen pizzas Choose a thin-based Margarita type and embellish with your own toppings – salami, olives, capers, mozzarella, basil and grilled or bottled peppers.

Frozen peas For those days when your vegetable rack is completely bare. Try them tossed with crispy bacon, shredded lettuce and a spoonful of cream. Or cook with pancetta or bacon, arborio rice, a softened onion and a splash of white wine to make *risi e bisi*.

Large raw prawns With saffron rice and peas they make a meal that's good enough for entertaining. Also good for stir-fries, or with Thai green curry paste and coconut milk, or sautéed in garlic butter.

Good sausages Visit a speciality butcher and stock up on good sausages. Freeze in portions and cook slowly from frozen. Serve with mash, slice and toss with pasta, or bake in the oven with whole garlic cloves and serve with canned black-eyed beans stewed with chopped tomatoes, harissa, thyme and a bay leaf.

Good ice cream For making quick and delicious desserts. Top with sauces, maple syrup, chopped nuts, or simply enjoy on its own.

F R E S H   H E R B S

Fresh herbs add instant flavour, fragrance and vibrance to any dish. Think of tomato and basil salad, *omelette fines herbes*, lamb grilled with rosemary, or a Mexican salsa heady with coriander. Dried herbs are not much of a substitute for the real thing in general cooking, and in fast cooking they are of minimal use since they are not cooked for long enough to allow their harsh flavour to mellow. So, instead of filling your shelves with jars of powdery dried herbs that don't get used, look for bundles of fresh herbs in your local greengrocer, prepacked in supermarkets or, even better, as growing plants that thrive on a kitchen window-sill.

F I V E   S T O R E C U P B O A R D   P A S T A S

Cook pasta in plenty of boiling salted water until *al dente* (tender but still slightly firm in the centre). Drain and toss with one of the following combinations.

✦ Crumbled dried chilli, crushed garlic, virgin olive oil
✦ Artichoke hearts, tuna, capers, chopped sun-dried tomatoes, canned chopped tomatoes
✦ Anchovies, sliced browned garlic, parsley, virgin olive oil
✦ Pan-fried pancetta or bacon, frozen peas, cream
✦ Mascarpone, chopped walnuts, Parmesan

FIVE STORECUPBOARD BAKED POTATO TOPPINGS

You'll need a microwave to 'bake' potatoes in less than 30 minutes. Crisp in the oven if you have extra time, and top with one of the following:

✦ Canned or bottled sweet peppers stewed *agrodolce* (sweet and sour) with onions, garlic, sugar and balsamic vinegar

✦ Hummus and yogurt

✦ Tuna, sweetcorn and mayonnaise

✦ Canned black-eyed beans and cream cheese with garlic

✦ Red kidney beans heated with canned tomatoes, a spoonful of tapenade or pesto and plenty of chilli

FIVE STORECUPBOARD SALADS

Try one of the following salad alternatives:

✦ Canned lentils, salami or crisp bacon and wholegrain mustard dressing

✦ Canned chick-peas, curry paste and yogurt dressing, with fresh coriander

✦ Peppered mackerel, boiled small potatoes (in their skins), wholegrain mustard, mayonnaise and cream or yogurt dressing

✦ Tuna, hard-boiled eggs, anchovies, gherkins, salad leaves and garlic dressing

✦ Bulghur wheat, French dressing, chopped onions, tomatoes and parsley

FIVE THINGS TO DO WITH A CAN OF CHOPPED TOMATOES

✦ *Barbecue chicken* Mix with tabasco sauce, Worcestershire sauce, brown sugar, mustard and garlic. Pour over small chicken drumsticks and bake in the oven at 230°C (450°F) mark 8 for 20-30 minutes.

✦ *Minestrone soup* Mix with diced vegetables, vegetable stock, cannellini beans and ditalini (or other soup pasta). Simmer until the vegetables are cooked. Serve topped with a spoonful of pesto and grated Parmesan.

✦ *Mexican rice* Cook with long-grain rice, vegetable stock, lots of garlic and chillies. Serve with refried beans, guacamole, soured cream and tortillas.

✦ *Curried eggs* Flavour with curry paste and fresh coriander. Simmer with a little cream until reduced. Serve with hard-boiled eggs.

✦ *Baked chicken with vegetables* Mix with chunky pieces of pepper and courgettes, whole garlic cloves, and a few black olives. Pour over chicken breast
fillets and bake in the oven at 230°C (450°F) mark 8 for 25 minutes. Add lots
of chopped fresh basil just before serving with rice.

T O P   T I P S   F O R   T H E   Q U I C K   C O O K

✦ An uncluttered kitchen will help things run smoothly. Likewise, a tidy pantry
or food cupboard will help you locate things in a hurry.

✦ Keep everyday basics like olive oil, salt and pepper next to the hob.

✦ If you're cooking pasta, put the water on to boil before you do anything else.

✦ Keep your food processor on the work surface (not tucked away in a cupboard) and use it to make dips, sauces, salsas, soup and pancake batter.

✦ Assemble everything before you start. It is really annoying to get halfway
through a recipe only to discover that something crucial is missing.

✦ Keep at least one good cook's knife and sharpen it regularly.

✦ Start onions softening while you chop other ingredients.

✦ A basic vinaigrette will keep in the fridge for weeks. Add herbs, garlic or
chillies as required. If you don't have time to make your own, buy supermarket dressing and embellish as above.

✦ Use the microwave for what it's good at. Remember that it will heat baked
beans, soften or melt butter, cook frozen peas, heat soup in a soup bowl, bake
potatoes (crisp in a hot oven once they're cooked), make all-in-one white
sauce, cook scrambled eggs in a bowl, melt equal quantities of plain chocolate and cream for a quick chocolate sauce, bring cold (sliced) tomatoes
sprinkled with oil to room temperature for salads, as well as thaw and reheat.

✦ Make double quantities and freeze half for another day. Good things to freeze
ahead are ragu or bolognese sauce, macaroni or cauliflower cheese, rich
tomato sauce, kedgeree.

✦ Train yourself to do several things at once. Don't sit and read the paper while
the rice cooks; instead get the sauce ready, warm the bread or make the salad.

NOTE There are some recipes in this book which require marinating. Although
this increases the overall time needed to more than 30 minutes, we have in-
cluded them because the recipes themselves are still quick to cook and prepare.

Soups,
Starters and
Light Meals

Tomato, Pepper and Orange Soup

PREPARATION TIME: 5 MINUTES
COOKING TIME: 10 MINUTES
SERVES 6
70 CALORIES PER SERVING

400 g (14 oz) can of pimientos (red peppers), drained

a few sprigs of fresh rosemary or
5 ml (1 level tsp) dried rosemary

10 ml (2 level tsp) caster sugar

1 litre (1¾ pints) tomato juice

300 ml (½ pint) chicken stock

450 ml (¾ pint) freshly squeezed orange juice

salt and pepper

orange slices and rosemary sprigs, to garnish

1 Put the pimientos, rosemary, sugar and half the tomato juice in a blender or food processor, and blend until smooth.

2 Sieve the mixture into a saucepan and stir in the stock, orange juice and remaining tomato juice. Season with salt and pepper.

3 Bring to the boil, then reduce the heat and simmer gently for about 10 minutes. Adjust the seasoning and serve, garnished with orange slices and rosemary sprigs.

Spinach Soup

PREPARATION TIME: 10 MINUTES
COOKING TIME: 15 MINUTES
SERVES 4
140 CALORIES PER SERVING

450 g (1 lb) spinach leaves

900 ml (1½ pints) vegetable stock

15 ml (1 tbsp) lemon juice

salt and pepper

a few drops of Tabasco

450 ml (¾ pint) buttermilk

To serve

60 ml (4 tbsp) double cream

croûtons

1 Put the spinach, stock and lemon juice in a large saucepan. Season with salt and pepper, and bring to the boil, then reduce the heat and simmer for 10 minutes.

2 Allow to cool slightly, then purée in a blender or food processor until smooth. Pass through a sieve and return to the pan.

3 Reheat gently with the Tabasco and buttermilk. Serve hot with a little cream swirled in and accompanied by croûtons.

Spicy Fish Soup

PREPARATION TIME: 15 MINUTES
COOKING TIME: 10 MINUTES
SERVES 4
225 CALORIES PER SERVING

---

45 ml (3 level tbsp) cornflour

---

a good pinch of five-spice powder

2.5 ml (½ level tsp) salt

---

225 g (8 oz) cod or haddock fillet, skinned, boned and cut
into thin strips

---

150 ml (¼ pint) sunflower oil

---

900 ml (1½ pints) good chicken stock

---

1 cm (½ inch) piece of fresh root ginger, peeled and chopped

---

125 g (4 oz) canned bamboo shoots, drained and cut into
strips

---

4 spring onions, trimmed and thinly sliced

---

1 garlic clove, skinned and crushed

---

15 ml (1 tbsp) light soy sauce

---

15 ml (1 tbsp) dry sherry

---

ground white pepper

---

125 g (4 oz) cooked peeled prawns

---

24 watercress leaves, to garnish

---

1 Mix the cornflour with the five-spice powder and salt, and coat the fish strips.

2 Heat the oil in a wok or large frying pan, add the fish strips and fry for 2 minutes or until crisp and golden. Drain on absorbent kitchen paper and reserve.

3 Heat the stock in a saucepan, with all the remaining ingredients, except the prawns and watercress leaves, and simmer for 2 minutes.

4 Add the reserved fried fish strips and prawns and heat through for 1 minute. Remove the pan from the heat, add the watercress and serve immediately.

Chicken and Coconut Soup

PREPARATION TIME: 15 MINUTES
COOKING TIME: 15 MINUTES
SERVES 4
360 CALORIES PER SERVING

15 cm (6 inch) lemon grass stalk

15 ml (1 tbsp) oil

225 g (8 oz) chicken breast, skinned and cut into strips

1 green chilli, deseeded and chopped

5 cm (2 inch) piece of fresh root ginger, peeled and finely sliced

600 ml (1 pint) coconut milk

300 ml (½ pint) chicken stock

15 ml (1 tbsp) Thai-style fish sauce

5 ml (1 tsp) light soy sauce

50 g (2 oz) oyster or button mushrooms, wiped and sliced

15-30 ml (1-2 level tbsp) torn fresh coriander leaves

1 Split the lemon grass stalk lengthways down the middle and finely slice.

2 Heat the oil in a saucepan, add the chicken and fry until the chicken turns from pink to white. Add the chilli, lemon grass and ginger, and continue cooking for 1 minute.

3 Stir in the coconut milk, stock, fish sauce and soy sauce. Bring to the boil, then reduce the heat and simmer gently for about 10 minutes or until the chicken breast strips are tender. Add the mushrooms and simmer for about 2 minutes or until just cooked. Just before serving, stir in the fresh coriander leaves.

Chicken Noodle Soup

PREPARATION TIME: 10 MINUTES
COOKING TIME: 20 MINUTES
SERVES 4
210 CALORIES PER SERVING

50 g (2 oz) shiitake or oyster mushrooms, thinly sliced

15 ml (1 tbsp) oil

1.2 litres (2 pints) chicken stock

60 ml (4 tbsp) dry or medium sherry

30 ml (2 tbsp) light soy sauce, or to taste

5 cm (2 inch) piece of fresh root ginger, peeled and crushed

125 g (4 oz) skinless chicken breast fillet, cut into strips

1 bunch of spring onions, trimmed and sliced diagonally into 2.5 cm (1 inch) lengths

50 g (2 oz) lean cooked ham, cut into strips

230 g (8 oz) can of bamboo shoots, drained and cut into strips

125 g (4 oz) Chinese egg noodles

salt and pepper

1 Heat the oil in a large frying pan, add the mushrooms and sauté gently for about 5 minutes or until softened. Remove from the pan and drain.

2 Put the stock in a large saucepan and bring to the boil. Add the sherry, soy sauce and ginger, lower the heat, and then add the chicken and spring onions. Cover and cook for 10 minutes or until the chicken is tender.

3 Add the ham and bamboo shoots to the soup with the noodles and mushrooms, and simmer for about 5 minutes or until the noodles are tender. Add salt and pepper to taste, with more soy sauce if liked. Serve immediately.

COOK'S TIP

Serve with prawn crackers to make a substantial starter for a Chinese-style meal.

Carpaccio of Salmon

PREPARATION TIME: 15 MINUTES
SERVES 10
200 CALORIES PER SERVING

550 g (1¼ lb) salmon fillet, skinned

225 g (8 oz) tomatoes, deseeded and finely chopped

1 bunch of fresh chives or spring onions, trimmed and cut
into 5 cm (2 inch) lengths

juice of 2 limes

100 ml (4 fl oz) olive oil

salt and pepper

lime wedges, to garnish

brown bread and butter, to serve

1 Cut the salmon into 20 slices. Place between sheets of oiled cling film and bat out thinly with a rolling pin until the slices are about the thickness of sliced smoked salmon.

2 Mix the tomatoes and chives with the lime juice, olive oil, and salt and pepper to taste.

3 Just before serving, arrange the salmon on individual serving plates and spoon the dressing over. Garnish with lime wedges and serve with brown bread and butter.

VARIATION

If the idea of eating raw salmon doesn't appeal to you, serve the same quantity of sliced smoked salmon instead. Alternatively, place the Carpaccio of Salmon in single layers in ovenproof dishes and cook in the oven at 220°C (425°F) mark 7 for about 5 minutes or until the salmon just turns opaque. Serve warm, garnished with lime.

Devilled Whitebait

PREPARATION TIME: 10 MINUTES
COOKING TIME: 10 MINUTES
SERVES 8
975 CALORIES PER SERVING

120 ml (8 level tbsp) plain flour

2.5 ml (½ level tsp) curry powder

2.5 ml (½ level tsp) ground ginger

2.5 ml (½ level tsp) cayenne pepper

salt

1.1 kg (2½ lb) whitebait

oil for deep-frying

25 g (1 oz) parsley sprigs

sea salt for sprinkling

lemon wedges, to serve

1 Sift the flour, curry powder, ginger, cayenne and salt together into a large plastic bag. Put a quarter of the whitebait into the bag and shake well to coat in the flour mixture. Lift the fish out and shake in a sieve to remove excess flour. Repeat with the remaining whitebait.

2 Heat the oil in a deep-fat fryer to 190°C (375°F) or until a 2.5 cm (1 inch) cube of bread will brown in the hot oil in 40 seconds. Put a single layer of whitebait into the frying basket and lower it into the oil. Fry for 2-3 minutes, shaking the basket occasionally. Tip out on to a warmed plate lined with absorbent kitchen paper. Fry the remaining whitebait in the same way.

3 Allow the oil temperature to reduce to about 185°C (365°F). Deep-fry the parsley for a few seconds. Drain on absorbent kitchen paper and sprinkle with salt.

4 Divide the whitebait between individual warmed serving plates. Scatter over the parsley and garnish with lemon wedges.

Devilled Prawns

PREPARATION TIME: 5 MINUTES
COOKING TIME: 6 MINUTES
SERVES 6
200 CALORIES PER SERVING

15 ml (1 tbsp) olive oil

125 g (4 oz) onion, skinned and finely chopped

2 garlic cloves, skinned and crushed

1.25 ml (¼ level tsp) each black pepper and salt

2.5 ml (½ level tsp) each dried oregano and thyme

15 ml (1 level tbsp) ground paprika

60 ml (4 tbsp) dry sherry

142 ml (5 fl oz) carton of double cream

400 g (14 oz) cooked peeled prawns

ground paprika, to garnish

1 Heat the oil in a frying pan, add the onion and garlic, and fry for 3-4 minutes or until softened.

2 Add the pepper, salt, herbs, paprika and sherry, and cook, stirring, for 1 minute.

3 Pour in the cream and bubble vigorously to reduce the sauce slightly.

4 Add the prawns and heat through for 1 minute. Serve immediately, sprinkled with paprika.

Bagna Cauda

PREPARATION TIME: 10 MINUTES
COOKING TIME: 2-3 MINUTES
SERVES 6
370 CALORIES PER SERVING

*Serve this warm dip in a dish that will retain the heat. Buy
ready-prepared crudités or pick a colour theme, such as red
and green, for vegetables which need little preparation -
radishes, cucumber, peppers, cherry tomatoes, etc. Offer a
selection of crisps and savouries, too.*

fresh vegetable crudités
142 ml (5 fl oz) carton of thick double cream
60 ml (4 tbsp) olive oil
2 garlic cloves, skinned
50 g (2 oz) can of anchovy fillets
125 g (4 oz) walnut pieces
salt and pepper
anchovy fillet and chopped walnuts, to garnish

1 Prepare the crudités, if necessary. Put all the remaining ingredients in a
blender or food processor and blend until quite smooth, reserving one
anchovy fillet for garnish.

2 Pour the mixture into a saucepan and warm through very gently, stirring continuously. Season with salt and pepper.

3 Serve warm accompanied by the vegetable crudités and garnished with the
reserved anchovy fillet and walnuts.

Sesame Mangetout with Prawns

PREPARATION TIME: 5 MINUTES
COOKING TIME: 10 MINUTES
SERVES 6
140 CALORIES PER SERVING

450 g (1 lb) mangetout, trimmed

salt and pepper

45 ml (3 level tbsp) sesame seeds

10 ml (2 tsp) vegetable oil

5 ml (1 tsp) sesame oil

1 garlic clove, skinned and crushed

125 g (4 oz) large cooked peeled prawns

50 g (2 oz) salted roasted cashew nuts

30 ml (2 tbsp) light soy sauce

warm naan bread (see Note), to serve (optional)

1 Cook the mangetout in boiling salted water for 1 minute. Drain, then rinse under cold running water to prevent further cooking.

2 Place the sesame seeds on a baking sheet and toast under the grill for about 5 minutes or until golden brown.

3 Heat the oils in a wok or large frying pan with the garlic. Stir in the mangetout, prawns, cashew nuts and soy sauce, and stir-fry for about 3 minutes. Add the sesame seeds and cook for a further 30 seconds.

4 Adjust the seasoning, then serve on warmed plates accompanied by warm naan bread, if wished.

NOTE

Naan bread is Indian flat bread, sometimes flavoured with herbs, which is available from large supermarkets. If you cannot find it, serve warm pitta bread instead.

Thai Fish Bites

PREPARATION TIME: 15 MINUTES
COOKING TIME: 10 MINUTES
MAKES 30
30 CALORIES PER BITE

550 g (1¼ lb) skinned cod fillet

30 ml (2 level tbsp) red curry paste

30 ml (2 tbsp) Thai-style fish sauce

2 eggs

15 basil leaves

grated rind of 1 lime

oil for deep-frying

chilli dipping sauce, to serve

1 Roughly chop the cod fillet and place in a blender or food processor with all the remaining ingredients, except the oil and chilli sauce. Blend for about 1 minute or until smooth.

2 With wet hands, shape the mixture into walnut-sized balls.

3 Heat the oil in a frying pan, and fry the fish bites in batches for 3-4 minutes or until golden brown and cooked through. Drain on absorbent kitchen paper. Place on a baking sheet and keep warm, uncovered, in a low oven until all the bites are cooked. Serve with a chilli dipping sauce.

Grilled Chicory with Pears and Hazelnuts

PREPARATION TIME: 10 MINUTES
COOKING TIME: 8-13 MINUTES
SERVES 4
170 CALORIES PER SERVING

2 large or 4 small heads of chicory

olive oil, for basting

1 ripe pear

30 ml (2 tbsp) hazelnut oil

7.5 ml (1½ level tsp) chopped fresh thyme

pepper

25 g (1 oz) hazelnuts, toasted and chopped

thyme sprigs, to garnish

crusty Italian bread, to serve

1 Halve the chicory heads lengthways and cut out the cores. Brush all over with olive oil. Place in a grill pan, cut side up, and cook under a very hot grill as near to the heat as possible for 3-4 minutes (2-3 minutes for smaller heads) or until just beginning to char and soften. Turn, baste with more oil and cook for a further 2-3 minutes (1-2 minutes for smaller heads).

2 Halve, core and slice the pear. Carefully turn the chicory again and top with the pear slices. Brush with hazelnut oil, sprinkle on the thyme, season with pepper and grill for 5-6 minutes (4-5 minutes for smaller heads). The chicory will be very soft, so transfer it carefully to warmed plates. Scatter with the hazelnuts, garnish with extra sprigs of thyme and drizzle with the remaining hazelnut oil. Serve with crusty Italian bread.

Felafel

PREPARATION TIME: 15 MINUTES
COOKING TIME: 8-12 MINUTES
SERVES 4-6
435-290 CALORIES PER SERVING

Serve these spicy chick-pea balls with a bowl of yogurt
flavoured with chopped fresh coriander or mint.

two 400 g (15 oz) cans of chick-peas, drained and rinsed
5 ml (1 level tsp) ground cumin
5 ml (1 level tsp) ground turmeric
5 ml (1 level tsp) cayenne pepper
5 ml (1 level tsp) salt
1 garlic clove, skinned and crushed
30 ml (2 tbsp) tahini (see page 28)
50 g (2 oz) fresh breadcrumbs
45 ml (3 level tbsp) chopped fresh coriander
plain flour for coating
oil for deep-frying

1 Put all the ingredients, except the flour and oil, in a blender or food processor and blend until the chick-peas are finely chopped but not puréed.

2 Turn the mixture into a large bowl and add about 30 ml (2 tbsp) water. Knead the mixture with your hands until it begins to cling together, adding a little extra water if necessary. With floured hands, shape the mixture into 20 walnut-sized balls. Slightly flatten each ball with the palm of your hand and coat in flour.

3 Heat the oil in a deep-fat fryer to 190°C (375°F) or until a 2.5 cm (1 inch) cube of bread will brown in the hot oil in 40 seconds. Fry the felafel in the hot oil, a few at a time, for 2-3 minutes or until golden brown. Drain on crumpled absorbent kitchen paper and serve hot.

Stir-fried Mushrooms with Cashew Nuts

PREPARATION TIME: 10 MINUTES
COOKING TIME: 5 MINUTES
SERVES 4
90 CALORIES PER SERVING

---

15 ml (1 tbsp) oil

---

25 g (1 oz) unsalted cashew nuts

---

225 g (8 oz) brown-cap mushrooms, wiped and sliced

---

15 ml (1 tbsp) lemon juice

---

60 ml (4 level tbsp) chopped fresh coriander or parsley

---

salt and pepper

---

15 ml (1 tbsp) single cream (optional)

---

warm crusty bread or rolls, to serve

---

1 Heat the oil in a frying pan, add the nuts and cook over a high heat for 2-3 minutes or until golden. Add the mushrooms and cook for a further 2-3 minutes or until tender, stirring frequently.

2 Stir in the lemon juice and coriander, season with salt and pepper, and bubble up. Remove from the heat and stir in the cream. Adjust the seasoning and serve with warm crusty bread or rolls.

Creamy Hummus

PREPARATION TIME: 5 MINUTES + CHILLING
SERVES 4
270 CALORIES PER SERVING

400 g (14 oz) can of chick-peas, drained and rinsed

1 garlic clove, skinned and crushed

75 ml (3 fl oz) light tahini (see Note)

15 ml (1 tbsp) olive oil

45 ml (3 tbsp) lemon juice

45-60 ml (3-4 level tbsp) Greek yogurt

salt and pepper

To serve

paprika

lemon wedges

black olives

bread sticks

1 Put the chick-peas in a blender or food processor with the remaining ingredients and 25 ml (1 fl oz) water. Blend until smooth, then taste and adjust the seasoning if necessary. Spoon the hummus into a serving dish, cover and chill for at least 20 minutes.

2 Sprinkle the hummus with paprika and serve with accompaniments.

NOTE

Tahini is a thick, creamy paste, made from ground sesame seeds and sesame oil, which has long been popular in the Middle East. Light and dark varieties are available; the dark version is made from unhusked sesame seeds and has a much stronger, bitter flavour. For this recipe, it is preferable to use one of the lighter blends, but if you already have a jar of dark tahini in your cupboard, reduce the quantity to about 30 ml (2 level tbsp).

Warm Salad of Mushrooms

Preparation time: 15 minutes
Cooking time: 10-12 minutes
Serves 6-8
280-210 calories per serving

selection of salad leaves

175 g (6 oz) young spinach leaves

175 g (6 oz) smoked streaky bacon

700 g (1½ lb) mushrooms (see Cook's Tip), wiped

90 ml (6 tbsp) olive oil

1 garlic clove, skinned and crushed (optional)

salt and pepper

25 ml (1½ tbsp) tarragon vinegar

1 Arrange the salad leaves and spinach on individual plates. Remove the rind from the bacon, then cut the bacon into thin strips. Cut the mushrooms into thick slices.

2 Heat a heavy-based frying pan and fry the bacon until the fat runs. Increase the heat and fry for 2-3 minutes or until crisp. Add the oil and mushrooms and cook over a high heat for 3-4 minutes or until the mushrooms are just tender. Add the garlic, if using, season with pepper, and cook for a minute longer.

3 Using a slotted spoon, remove the mushrooms from the pan and scatter them over the salad leaves. Quickly add the vinegar to the juice remaining in the pan and boil rapidly for 2 minutes. Season with salt and pepper. Pour the warm dressing over the salads and serve immediately.

COOK'S TIP

If possible, use a mixture of wild mushrooms for this salad. Otherwise a mixture of cultivated oyster, shiitake and cup mushrooms works well.

Asparagus with Coriander Hollandaise

PREPARATION TIME: 25 MINUTES
COOKING TIME: 10 MINUTES
SERVES 4
295 CALORIES PER SERVING

450 g (1 lb) asparagus

salt

15 ml (1 tbsp) lemon juice

blanched lemon rind strips and chervil sprigs, to garnish

For the sauce

125 g (4 oz) unsalted butter, diced

25 ml (1½ level tbsp) coriander seeds, crushed and lightly toasted

25 ml (1½ tbsp) lemon juice

10 ml (2 tsp) white wine vinegar

2 egg yolks

pinch of sugar

pinch of salt

1 To make the sauce, melt the butter in a saucepan, add the coriander seeds and warm gently until the butter just begins to bubble. Remove from the heat, cover and leave to infuse for 20 minutes.

2 Meanwhile, scrape the asparagus stalks and remove the woody ends. Tie the asparagus in two equal bundles. Stand them in a saucepan of boiling salted water, to which the lemon juice has been added, so that they stand upright; the tips should be out of the water.

3 Cover with a lid or a dome of foil and cook gently for about 10 minutes or until tender, depending on the size of the spears.

4 For the sauce, put the lemon juice and vinegar in a saucepan and bring to the boil. Gently reheat the coriander butter until just beginning to foam.

5 Put the egg yolks, sugar and salt in a blender and blend briefly, then, with the motor running, slowly pour in the lemon juice and vinegar mixture. When it has all been absorbed, slowly pour in the coriander butter, with the motor still running.

6 Drain the asparagus well and arrange on warmed serving plates. Spoon the coriander hollandaise over the asparagus. Garnish with strips of lemon rind and sprigs of chervil.

Italian Artichokes

PREPARATION TIME: 10 MINUTES
COOKING TIME: 25-30 MINUTES
SERVES 4-6
390-260 CALORIES PER SERVING

225 g (8 oz) baby new potatoes, scrubbed

salt and pepper

125 g (4 oz) French beans, trimmed

30 ml (2 tbsp) olive oil

6 streaky bacon rashers, derinded and chopped

30 ml (2 level tbsp) plain flour

300 ml (½ pint) vegetable stock

two 400 g (14 oz) cans of artichoke hearts, drained and halved

a squeeze of lemon juice

45 ml (3 level tbsp) chopped fresh parsley

15 ml (1 tbsp) cream (optional)

chopped fresh parsley, to garnish

1 Cook the potatoes in boiling salted water for 15-20 minutes or until tender. Cook the French beans in a separate pan of boiling salted water for 3-5 minutes or until just tender.

2 Heat the oil in a shallow pan, add the bacon and cook for 3-5 minutes or until cooked and golden brown. Stir in the flour and cook for 1 minute, stirring. Gradually add the stock, bring to the boil slowly and cook, stirring, until the mixture thickens.

3 Add the potatoes, French beans, artichokes, lemon juice, parsley and cream, if using, and season with salt and pepper. Serve warm, garnished with parsley.

Bruschetta

PREPARATION TIME: 5 MINUTES
COOKING TIME: 10 MINUTES
SERVES 6
320 CALORIES PER SERVING

---

1 garlic clove, skinned and halved

---

1 loaf of ciabatta bread, sliced diagonally

---

olive oil

---

50 g (2 oz) fresh white breadcrumbs

---

225 g (8 oz) cleaned and cooked squid rings

---

12 cooked peeled Mediterranean prawns

---

125 g (4 oz) cooked shelled mussels

---

freshly ground black pepper

---

sprigs of fresh marjoram

---

1 Rub the garlic over one side of each slice of bread. Heat a little olive oil in a frying pan and gently fry the breadcrumbs. Remove from the pan. Put the seafood in the pan and warm through for 1-2 minutes.

2 Meanwhile, drizzle a little olive oil over the bread slices and grill until lightly toasted on both sides. Arrange on individual plates and pile the seafood on top. Scatter over the breadcrumbs. Drizzle with a little olive oil, season with pepper and finish with marjoram.

VARIATIONS

Parma ham Toast the bread, as above, and spread with a tomato base made by mixing a few chopped sun-dried tomatoes into some passata. Top with slices of Parma ham and red onion, orange segments and olives. Finish with thyme.

Chorizo Quickly sauté slices of red and yellow pepper and slivers of chilli. Toast the bread and spread with a tomato base as for Parma ham above. Top with folded slices of chorizo, the peppers and chilli. Finish with flat-leaf parsley.

Mozzarella Toast garlic bread, as above, and top with sautéed chopped tomatoes, chunks of mozzarella, basil and one black olive per slice.

Chicken Liver Crostini

PREPARATION TIME: 20 MINUTES
COOKING TIME: 5 MINUTES
SERVES 4-6
550-365 CALORIES PER SERVING

*Try to use a thin 'French-style' baguette for making the
bread croûtes. The larger, fatter versions are rather cumber-
some, too crusty and open-textured. If you can't get hold of
a baguette, use slices of white bread cut into neat triangles.*

450 g (1 lb) chicken livers
½ baguette
50-75 g (2-3 oz) butter
1-2 large garlic cloves, skinned
50 g (2 oz) French beans, mangetout or sugar snap peas, trimmed
selection of salad leaves, such as batavia, oakleaf lettuce and radicchio
15 ml (1 level tbsp) wholegrain mustard
45 ml (3 tbsp) raspberry or garlic vinegar
75 ml (5 tbsp) olive oil
salt and pepper
chopped fresh parsley, to garnish

1 Trim the chicken livers, cut each one into 3-4 pieces and set aside. Cut 12 thin diagonal slices from the baguette.

2 Heat 50 g (2 oz) butter in a frying pan and fry the bread in batches on both sides until golden brown and crisp, adding more butter to the pan if necessary. Remove from the pan and drain on crumpled absorbent kitchen paper.

3 Cut one garlic clove in half and rub over both sides of the bread. If you like a pronounced garlic flavour, repeat this process with a second clove.

4 Blanch the French beans, mangetout or sugar snap peas in boiling salted water. Cook French beans for 2 minutes; mangetout for 30 seconds; sugar snap peas for 1 minute. Drain and refresh under cold running water then drain thoroughly.

5 Arrange the salad leaves on individual serving plates and scatter the blanched vegetables on top.

6 In a bowl, whisk together the mustard, 15 ml (1 tbsp) vinegar and 60 ml (4 tbsp) olive oil. Season with salt and pepper, pour over the salad leaves and carefully toss each portion to coat all the leaves. Position two or three croûtes on each portion of dressed salad leaves.

7 Add the remaining olive oil to any butter left in the frying pan and heat. Add the chicken livers and cook swiftly over a high heat for 3-4 minutes; they should be brown on the outside but still pink in the centre. Using a slotted spoon, remove the cooked livers from the pan and pile on top of the croûtes.

8 Quickly add the remaining vinegar to the pan and heat gently, scraping up any sediment from the bottom of the pan. Season with salt and pepper, then pour over the chicken livers. Scatter with plenty of chopped parsley and serve immediately.

Quick Snack Ideas

Bread is great for making starters and snacks at the last minute. Try some of the following:

✦ Sauté thinly sliced red onions in a little oil until soft. Spread over toasted olive ciabatta. Top with creamy goat's cheese and season with thyme, salt and pepper. Grill until the cheese melts.

✦ Toast sun-dried tomato or olive bread and cut into large cubes. Make a salad with hard-boiled eggs, new potatoes, avocados, cherry tomatoes and crisp lettuce. Add the bread cubes and toss with herb, garlic or chilli dressing.

✦ Using thick slices of bread, make a mozzarella and onion sandwich, smearing one slice of bread with a little harissa sauce. Butter the outsides of the sandwich and grill under a moderate heat until browned on the outside and the cheese has melted. Serve while still warm with salad leaves.

✦ Brush thin aubergine slices with oil, then cook under a hot grill. Rub thick slices of toasted sourdough bread with a cut garlic clove, then spread with a thin layer of bottled tapenade. Add generous amounts of rocket or watercress, then top with the aubergine. Season and drizzle with virgin olive oil.

✦ Place a whole focaccia on a baking sheet and slash its surface. Push some raisins and small seedless grapes into the cuts, and drizzle with a little olive oil, chopped rosemary and coarse sea salt, then bake in the oven at 200°C (400°F) mark 6 for 10 minutes.

✦ Toast slices of baguette on one side, then spread with garlic butter and grill until melted and golden. Cool a little and cut into chunks. Whizz together 50 g (2 oz) sun-dried tomatoes with 150 ml (¼ pint) olive oil, 60 ml (4 tbsp) red wine vinegar, 30 ml (2 tbsp) tomato paste, 60 ml (4 tbsp) freshly grated Parmesan, a few drops of Tabasco, a pinch of caster sugar and a handful of parsley. Toss the bread in the dressing and serve within the hour.

Eggs and
Cheese

Omelette

PREPARATION TIME: 5 MINUTES
COOKING TIME: 1 - 1 $^1/_2$ MINUTES
SERVES 1
390 CALORIES PER SERVING

2-3 eggs

salt and pepper

15 ml (1 tbsp) milk or water

butter or margarine for frying

1 Whisk the eggs just enough to break them down; over-beating spoils the texture of the omelette. Season with salt and pepper and add the milk or water.

2 Place an omelette or non-stick frying pan over a gentle heat and, when it is hot, add a generous knob of butter and heat until it is foaming but not brown.

3 Add the beaten eggs. Stir gently with a fork or wooden spatula, drawing the mixture from the sides to the centre as it sets, and letting the liquid egg in the centre run to the sides. When the eggs have set, stop stirring and cook for a further 30 seconds-1 minute or until the omelette is golden brown underneath and still creamy on top. Don't over-cook or it will be tough.

4 If making a filled omelette, add the filling at this point. Tilt the pan away from you slightly and use a palette knife to fold over a third of the omelette to the centre, then fold over the opposite third. Slide the omelette out on to a warmed plate, letting it flip over so that the folded sides are underneath. Serve at once.

Omelette Fillings

+ FINES HERBES: Add 15 ml (1 level tbsp) finely chopped fresh chervil, chives and tarragon, or a large pinch of dried mixed herbs, to the beaten egg mixture before cooking.

+ TOMATO: Skin and chop 1-2 tomatoes and fry in a little butter for 5 minutes or until soft and pulpy. Put in the centre of the omelette before folding.

+ CHEESE: Grate 40 g (1½ oz) cheese. Sprinkle half on the omelette before folding. Sprinkle the rest over the finished omelette.

+ MUSHROOM: Thickly slice about 50 g (2 oz) mushrooms and cook in butter until soft. Put in the centre of the omelette before folding. (When available, use wild mushrooms.)

+ CURRIED VEGETABLE: Roughly chop leftover vegetables, such as potato, green beans, broad beans or parsnips. Fry in oil with about 2.5 ml (½ level tsp) curry powder and a little crushed garlic. Put in the centre of the omelette before folding.

+ LOVAGE AND BLUE CHEESE: Add 10 ml (2 level tsp) finely chopped fresh lovage to the beaten egg mixture. Cut 25-50 g (1-2 oz) Blue Cheshire, Blue Stilton or Blue Wensleydale cheese into thin slices and scatter over the omelette before folding.

+ GOAT'S CHEESE: Soften about 25 g (1 oz) mild goat's cheese and blend with a little fromage frais. Season with salt and pepper and put in the centre of the omelette before folding.

+ PRAWN: Allow 50 g (2 oz) cooked peeled prawns per omelette. Sprinkle the prawns and a little chopped fresh tarragon in the centre of the omelette before folding.

+ SMOKED SALMON: Combine 25 g (1 oz) chopped smoked salmon with a little chopped fresh dill and 15 ml (1 tbsp) soured cream. Put in the centre of the omelette before folding.

Courgette and Bacon Frittata

PREPARATION TIME: 10 MINUTES
COOKING TIME: 12 MINUTES
SERVES 4
160 CALORIES PER SERVING

This delicious variation on an omelette is quick and easy to prepare - ideal for supper with friends.

15 ml (1 tbsp) oil
450 g (1 lb) courgettes, trimmed and thickly sliced
125 g (4 oz) smoked streaky bacon, derinded and roughly chopped
50 g (2 oz) onion, skinned and roughly chopped
30 ml (2 level tbsp) chopped fresh thyme
15 ml (1 level tbsp) chopped fresh rosemary
2 eggs
salt and pepper
chopped fresh herbs, to garnish

1 Heat the oil in a non-stick 20.5-25.5 cm (8-10 inch) frying pan, add the courgettes, bacon and onion, and fry for 4-5 minutes, stirring continuously, until just beginning to soften and turn golden brown.

2 Whisk together the thyme, rosemary and eggs. Season with salt and pepper and pour over the courgette mixture. Leave to set over a low heat for 2-3 minutes. Serve immediately, cut into wedges and sprinkled with fresh herbs.

Baked Ham Tortilla

PREPARATION TIME: 10 MINUTES
COOKING TIME: 20-25 MINUTES
SERVES 4
360 CALORIES PER SERVING

45 ml (3 tbsp) olive oil
1 onion, skinned and chopped
2 garlic cloves, skinned and crushed
225 g (8 oz) gammon, diced
335 g (12 oz) tomatoes, skinned, deseeded and diced
225 g (8 oz) green beans, trimmed and cut into 2.5 cm (1 inch) lengths
6 eggs
salt and pepper

1 Heat the oil in a saucepan, add the onion, and cook over a moderate heat for 5 minutes or until softened. Add the garlic and gammon, and cook for 4-5 minutes, stirring frequently, until beginning to brown.

2 Add the tomatoes and cook gently until softened, then stir in the beans and simmer for about 3 minutes or until just tender. Transfer the mixture to a buttered, shallow baking dish.

3 Break the eggs into a bowl, season with salt and pepper, then beat two or three times with a fork, just to break up the yolks and mix very lightly.

4 Pour the egg mixture into the baking dish and bake in the oven at 200°C (400°F) mark 6 for 15-20 minutes or until set. Serve at once.

Egg Fried Rice

PREPARATION TIME: 10 MINUTES
COOKING TIME: 20 MINUTES
SERVES 6
420 CALORIES PER SERVING

*If serving this as a main meal, add a few more vegetables
and increase the nuts to 125 g (4 oz).*

450 g (1 lb) long-grain rice
salt
about 30 ml (2 tbsp) oil
1 large onion, skinned and chopped
1 green chilli, deseeded and chopped
2 large carrots, peeled and coarsely grated
1 green pepper, deseeded and finely chopped
4 spring onions, trimmed and chopped
50 g (2 oz) unsalted cashew nuts or peanuts (optional)
2 eggs, beaten
5 ml (1 level tsp) sugar
30 ml (2 tbsp) light soy sauce

1 Cook the rice in boiling salted water for about 10 minutes or until just tender. Drain the rice, rinse with boiling water, then spread out on a large plate or tray while cooking the vegetables.

2 Heat the oil in a wok or very large frying pan. Add the onion, chilli, carrots and green pepper, and stir-fry for 3-4 minutes or until the vegetables are softened. Add the spring onions and nuts, if using, and fry for 1 minute. Pour in the egg in a thin stream, stirring all the time so that it breaks up into small pieces. When all the egg has set, add the rice, sugar and soy sauce, and continue cooking, stirring all the time, until the rice is heated through. Add a little extra oil if the rice starts to stick. Serve immediately.

Soufflé Welsh Rarebits

PREPARATION TIME: 10 MINUTES
COOKING TIME: 20 MINUTES
SERVES 4
280 CALORIES PER SERVING

4 slices of wholemeal bread

about 25 g (1 oz) butter

15 ml (1 level tbsp) poppy seeds

15 ml (1 level tbsp) plain flour

150 ml (¼ pint) semi-skimmed milk

5 ml (1 level tsp) Dijon mustard

5 ml (1 tsp) Worcestershire sauce

125 g (4 oz) Edam or Gouda cheese, grated

2 eggs, separated

parsley sprigs, to garnish

1 Spread the slices of bread lightly with butter. Sprinkle with poppy seeds and bake in the oven at 190°C (375°F) mark 5 for 5 minutes.

2 Melt 15 g (½ oz) butter in a saucepan, stir in the flour and cook for 1 minute. Gradually stir in the milk and bring to the boil, stirring. Cook, stirring, over a low heat until thickened.

3 Remove from the heat and beat in the mustard, Worcestershire sauce, grated cheese and egg yolks.

4 Whisk the egg whites until stiff, then fold into the cheese mixture.

5 Spoon the mixture on top of the bread slices and return to the oven for a further 15 minutes or until puffed and golden. Serve immediately, garnished with parsley sprigs.

Cheese Fondue

PREPARATION TIME: **10** MINUTES
COOKING TIME: ABOUT **10** MINUTES
SERVES **4**
455 CALORIES PER SERVING

1 large garlic clove, skinned and halved
10 ml (2 level tsp) cornflour
45 ml (3 tbsp) Kirsch
200 ml (7 fl oz) dry white wine
15 ml (1 tbsp) lemon juice
200 g (7 oz) Gruyère cheese, grated
200 g (7 oz) Emmental cheese, grated
pepper
crusty bread, to serve

1 Rub the halved garlic clove around the inside of a fondue pan (or a heavy-based saucepan).

2 Blend the cornflour to a smooth paste with the Kirsch. Put the wine, lemon juice and grated cheeses in the pan with the blended cornflour and bring slowly to the boil, stirring all the time. Reduce the heat and simmer gently for 3-4 minutes, stirring frequently. Season with pepper.

3 Set the pan over the fondue burner at the table. Serve with plenty of bite-sized chunks of crusty bread for dipping.

COOK'S TIP

If you do not own a fondue set, transfer the fondue to a warmed serving dish and keep warm over a heated serving tray at the table.

Glamorgan Sausages

PREPARATION TIME: **10** MINUTES
COOKING TIME: **5** MINUTES
MAKES **8**
100 CALORIES PER SAUSAGE

---

175 g (6 oz) fresh breadcrumbs

---

125 g (4 oz) Caerphilly or Cheddar cheese, grated

---

1 small leek, trimmed and very finely chopped

---

15 ml (1 level tbsp) very finely chopped fresh parsley

---

large pinch of mustard powder

---

salt and pepper

---

1 egg, beaten

---

about 30 ml (2 tbsp) milk

---

plain flour for coating

---

oil for frying or grilling

---

1 In a large bowl, mix together the breadcrumbs, cheese, leek, parsley and mustard, and season with salt and pepper. Add the egg and mix thoroughly, then add enough milk to bind the mixture together.

2 Divide the mixture into 8 and shape into sausages.

3 If shallow frying, roll the sausages in flour to coat. Heat a little oil in a frying pan, add the sausages and fry for about 5 minutes or until golden brown. To grill, lightly brush the sausages with oil and cook under a hot grill for 3-4 minutes or until golden brown, turning occasionally. Serve hot immediately, or leave to cool and serve cold.

Deep-fried Camembert with Rhubarb Sauce

PREPARATION TIME: 15 MINUTES
COOKING TIME: 15 MINUTES
SERVES 4
540 CALORIES PER SERVING

8 Camembert cheese portions

1 large egg (size 1)

salt and pepper

125 g (4 oz) fine fresh breadcrumbs

sunflower oil for deep-frying

green salad leaves, to garnish

For the sauce

225 g (8 oz) rhubarb, trimmed and cut into pieces

40 g (1½ oz) sugar

1.25 ml (¼ level tsp) ground ginger

salt and pepper

1 To make the sauce, put the rhubarb and sugar in a saucepan with 15 ml (1 tbsp) water. Cover the pan and cook over a low heat for 10 minutes or until the rhubarb is very soft.

2 Remove the pan from the heat and leave to cool slightly. Tip the rhubarb and liquid into a blender or food processor, and blend until smooth. Stir in the ginger, and season with salt and pepper, then return to the pan and heat through gently.

3 Meanwhile, trim off the rind from the Camembert portions. Beat the egg with salt and pepper to taste and pour on to a large plate. Spread out the breadcrumbs on another plate. Dip the Camembert portions first in egg, then in breadcrumbs. Repeat the process, dipping them carefully a second time.

4 Heat the oil in a deep-fat fryer to 190°C (375°F) or until a 2.5 cm (1 inch) cube of bread will brown in the hot oil in 40 seconds. Fry the Camembert portions, four at a time, for about 2 minutes or until crisp and golden. Drain on absorbent kitchen paper and serve at once with the sauce. Garnish with salad.

Chèvre en Croûte

PREPARATION TIME: 5 MINUTES
COOKING TIME: 12 MINUTES
SERVES 6
125 CALORIES PER SERVING

½ short baguette
15-30 ml (1-2 tbsp) hazelnut oil
1 small garlic clove, skinned and crushed
125 g (4 oz) chèvre log, about 2.5 cm (1 inch) in diameter
paprika for sprinkling
6 thyme sprigs

1 Cut six 1 cm (½ inch) thick slices from the baguette. Mix the hazelnut oil with the garlic, and brush over both sides of the slices. Place on a baking sheet and bake in the oven at 180°C (350°F) mark 4 for about 5 minutes.

2 Cut the chèvre into six slices, place one on each baguette slice and top with a sprinkling of paprika and a sprig of thyme.

3 Return the croûtes to the oven for a further 7 minutes or until the cheese is soft and spongy. Serve warm.

Egg and Bacon Baguette with Pan-fried Tomatoes

PREPARATION TIME: **10** MINUTES
COOKING TIME: **20** MINUTES
SERVES **4**
520 CALORIES PER SERVING

450 g (1 lb) cherry tomatoes, halved

2 garlic cloves, skinned and crushed

black pepper

1 baguette

60 ml (4 level tbsp) mayonnaise

15 ml (1 tbsp) olive oil

275 g (10 oz) thinly cut rindless streaky bacon

30 ml (2 level tbsp) chopped fresh parsley

4 eggs

1 small frisée lettuce

1 Mix the tomatoes and garlic in a bowl, and season well with black pepper.

2 Cut the bread into four lengths and slice each piece in half but not all the way through. Open out the pieces and spread the cut sides with 15 ml (1 level tbsp) mayonnaise, then toast the cut sides under a hot grill. Keep warm, covered, under a low grill.

3 Heat the oil in a non-stick frying pan and fry the bacon in two batches until crisp and golden brown. Remove from the pan and keep warm. Quickly fry the tomatoes in the bacon fat for about 1 minute, then stir in the parsley.

4 Lightly poach the eggs.

5 Top the baguette pieces with frisée, bacon, warm tomatoes and an egg. Grind over black pepper to serve.

Quick and Easy Cheese Ideas

Don't throw away small pieces of leftover cheese – try using them up in the following ways:

✦ For a substantial supper dish, crumble a little Stilton and stir into a creamy broccoli or cauliflower soup just before serving. Reheat gently without boiling.

✦ Mash Stilton with a fork and mix with lots of chopped watercress and a spoonful or two of crème fraîche or lemon mayonnaise. Sandwich with wholegrain bread.

✦ Sauté sliced leeks and crushed garlic in olive oil. Stir in thin slices of Brie to serve as a delicious snack/supper or as a vegetable accompaniment.

✦ Coarsely grate some carrots, a little onion and some mature Cheddar cheese. Moisten with French dressing and serve as a salad or as a topping for jacket potatoes.

✦ Warm 100 ml (4 fl oz) dry cider with 125 g (4 oz) grated Cheddar or other hard cheese until evenly blended. Stir in 5 ml (1 level tsp) wholegrain mustard with seasoning to taste. Thicken with about 10 ml (2 level tsp) cornflour, mixed to a paste with a little cold water, and spoon over thick slices of toasted ciabatta bread or baguette. Flash under the grill to serve.

✦ Mash together equal quantities of Stilton or soft cheese with garlic and herbs, and butter. Spread thickly over chunks of crusty bread, wrap in foil and bake at 200°C (400°F) mark 6 for 15 minutes. Serve piping hot with soup.

+ Drain a 390 g (14 oz) can of artichoke hearts and halve or quarter. Place in a gratin dish, brush with a little oil and grill for 2-3 minutes or until warm. Meanwhile, mix 150 ml (¼ pint) mayonnaise with 10 ml (2 level tsp) Dijon mustard, 75 g (3 oz) grated Edam or Cheddar cheese and seasoning. Spoon over the artichokes. Sprinkle with a little more cheese, then place under a hot grill for 4-5 minutes or until golden. Serve with warm wholemeal bread. Serves 4.

+ For a special breakfast or lunch dish, shave or grate a small amount of Parmesan cheese and add to scrambled eggs with shreds of smoked salmon or leftover ham.

+ Toss hot pasta or rice with coarsely grated cheese to serve as a side dish.

+ *Croque monsieur* Make a Gruyère, ham and mustard sandwich. Spread the outsides with butter and fry until golden and the cheese melted. For a *croque madame*, top with a poached or fried egg.

Meat

Beef Stir-fry with Beans and Peanuts

PREPARATION TIME: 15 MINUTES
COOKING TIME: 10 MINUTES
SERVES 4
440 CALORIES PER SERVING

450 g (1 lb) rump or sirloin steak

1 egg white

about 60 ml (4 level tbsp) cornflour

225 g (8 oz) French beans, topped, tailed and halved

75 ml (5 level tbsp) groundnut or vegetable oil

1 bunch of spring onions, trimmed and cut diagonally into chunky slices

4 celery sticks, trimmed and cut diagonally into slices

1 garlic clove, skinned and crushed

30 ml (2 tbsp) dark soy sauce

300 ml (½ pint) beef stock

60 ml (4 tbsp) dry sherry

15 ml (1 tbsp) sweet chilli sauce (optional)

25 g (1 oz) roasted unsalted peanuts

celery leaves, to garnish

1 Trim the steak of excess fat and cut the meat into very thin strips. Beat the egg white with a fork until slightly frothy. Dip the steak strips into the egg white and then into the cornflour. Keep to one side.

2 Blanch the beans in boiling water for 2 minutes, then drain well and reserve.

3 Heat 30 ml (2 tbsp) of the oil in a wok or large frying pan, add the onions, celery, garlic and beans, and stir-fry for 3 minutes. Remove from the pan and reserve.

4 Add the remaining oil to the pan, add the steak strips, and stir-fry for 2 minutes. Stir in the soy sauce, stock, sherry and chilli sauce, if using, and mix well.

5 Return the vegetables to the pan and heat through, stirring all the time. Transfer the mixture to a serving dish, scatter with peanuts and garnish with celery leaves.

Pizzaiola Steak

PREPARATION TIME: 15 MINUTES
COOKING TIME: 5-10 MINUTES
SERVES 4
275 CALORIES PER SERVING

4 thin rump steaks
60 ml (4 tbsp) olive oil
2 garlic cloves, skinned and crushed
salt and pepper
450 g (1 lb) firm red tomatoes, skinned and chopped
45 ml (3 level tbsp) chopped fresh basil
15 ml (1 level tbsp) chopped fresh parsley
basil sprigs, to garnish

1 Trim excess fat from the steaks. Heat the oil in a large frying pan, add the steaks and fry quickly over a high heat for 2-3 minutes or until browned on both sides. Add the garlic, season with salt and pepper, and fry for 30 seconds.

2 Add the tomatoes and herbs, and cook for 3-5 minutes or until the tomatoes are softened and the juices reduced. Adjust the seasoning and serve at once, garnished with basil sprigs.

Steak au Poivre

PREPARATION TIME: 10 MINUTES
COOKING TIME: 6-12 MINUTES
SERVES 4
515 CALORIES PER SERVING

---

4 sirloin, rump or fillet steaks

---

30 ml (2 level tbsp) black or green peppercorns, coarsely
crushed

---

25 g (1 oz) butter or margarine

---

15 ml (1 tbsp) oil

---

salt

---

30 ml (2 tbsp) brandy

---

142 ml (5 fl oz) carton of double cream

---

1 Trim excess fat from the steaks, then place on the crushed peppercorns and press hard to encrust the surface of the meat. Turn to encrust the other side.

2 Heat the butter and oil in a frying pan and fry the steaks for 2 minutes on each side. Reduce the heat and continue cooking until cooked to taste. Season with salt.

3 Remove the steaks from the pan and keep warm. Add the brandy to the pan, remove from the heat and set it alight.

4 When the flames have died down, stir in the cream. Reheat gently, then pour over the steaks and serve immediately.

Green Beef Curry

PREPARATION TIME: 5 MINUTES
COOKING TIME: 10 MINUTES
SERVES 4
350 CALORIES PER SERVING

700 g (1½ lb) rump steak
15 ml (1 tbsp) oil
15 ml (1 level tbsp) green curry paste
2.5 ml (½ level tsp) ground cinnamon
15 ml (1 tbsp) Thai-style fish sauce
150 ml (¼ pint) coconut milk
grated rind of ½ lime
5 ml (1 level tsp) soft brown sugar
shredded Kaffir lime leaves (see Note) or coriander leaves, to garnish
fragrant rice, to serve

1 Trim the steak of any fat and cut into finger-length strips. Heat the oil in a wok or frying pan and fry the meat in batches over a high heat to give it a good brown colour. Add more oil if necessary.

2 Return the meat to the pan, add the remaining ingredients, and cook, stirring, for 3 minutes or until the sauce has reduced slightly and the meat is tender. Garnish with shredded Kaffir lime or coriander leaves and serve with fragrant rice.

NOTE

Kaffir lime leaves are used like bay leaves in Thai cooking. They give a sour/sharp, lemon/lime flavour. They can be found in Oriental food shops and freeze well.

Sesame Beef Salad

PREPARATION TIME: 20 MINUTES + MARINATING
COOKING TIME: 10 MINUTES
SERVES 6
215 CALORIES PER SERVING

This is a very quick recipe as the ingredients can be prepared at least 24 hours in advance and cooked just before serving.

30 ml (2 tbsp) soy sauce
30 ml (2 tbsp) Worcestershire sauce
30 ml (2 level tbsp) soft brown sugar
10 ml (2 level tsp) tomato purée
5 ml (1 tsp) lemon juice
15 ml (1 tbsp) white wine vinegar
20 ml (4 level tsp) sesame seeds
oil
2 garlic cloves, skinned and crushed
salt and pepper
700 g (1½ lb) rump steak
6 celery sticks
1 bunch of spring onions
1 small cucumber
naan bread (see page 23) or pitta bread, to serve

1 Mix the first seven ingredients together in a bowl with 30 ml (2 tbsp) oil and the garlic. Season with salt and pepper. Trim excess fat from the steak and slice the meat into strips 5 mm (¼ inch) thick and 5 cm (2 inches) long. Stir the strips into the marinade, cover and refrigerate for at least 3 hours or until ready to cook.

2 Cut the celery, spring onions and cucumber (discarding the seeds) into thin matchsticks. Refrigerate in a polythene bag until ready to use.

3 Heat a little oil in a large wok or non-stick frying pan until the oil begins to smoke. Lift the steak strips from the marinade and fry in small batches until they are well browned. Place them in a large bowl.

4 Add the rest of the marinade to the pan and boil until reduced to a syrup. Pour over the steak strips. Either stir all the vegetables in with the steak or serve separately, accompanied by slices of warm naan or pitta bread.

Spicy Burgers

PREPARATION TIME: 15 MINUTES
COOKING TIME: 10 MINUTES
SERVES 4
230 CALORIES PER SERVING

Serve these delicious burgers in pitta bread pockets with fried onions, cucumber and mint leaves.

450 g (1 lb) lean minced beef
3 spring onions, trimmed and chopped
1 garlic clove, skinned and crushed
15 ml (1 level tbsp) each ground coriander and cumin
1 egg, beaten
30 ml (2 level tbsp) each chopped fresh parsley and coriander
15 ml (1 tbsp) Tabasco or chilli sauce
salt and pepper
oil

1 Put the minced beef in a bowl with all the other ingredients, except the oil. Mix well and divide into eight burgers.

2 Brush the burgers lightly with oil and grill or fry for about 5 minutes on each side or until cooked through. Serve immediately.

Pan-fried Steaks with Herby Potatoes

PREPARATION TIME: 10 MINUTES
COOKING TIME: 15 MINUTES
SERVES 4
320 CALORIES PER SERVING

---

700 g (1½ lb) small new potatoes, halved

---

125 g (4 oz) shallots or onions, skinned and finely chopped

---

salt

---

30 ml (2 tbsp) olive oil

---

1 garlic clove, skinned and crushed

---

125 g (4 oz) dolcelatte or cambazola cheese, diced

---

15 ml (1 level tbsp) chopped fresh thyme

---

4 sirloin, rump or fillet steaks, trimmed

---

fresh watercress, to garnish

---

1 Cook the potatoes and shallots together in boiling salted water for 4-5 minutes or until the potatoes are almost tender. Drain well.

2 Toss the potatoes and shallots in the olive oil with the garlic. Place in a flat, heatproof dish or baking sheet. Cook under a hot grill for 5-7 minutes or until crisp and brown. Dot with the cheese and return to the grill for 1-2 minutes or until melted and golden. Sprinkle with chopped thyme.

3 Pan-fry the steaks to your liking and serve them immediately, garnished with watercress, and accompanied by the herby potatoes.

COOK'S TIP

Before pan-frying the steaks, tie a rasher of rindless, smoked streaky bacon around them to give a delicious smoky flavour.

Italian-style Veal Kebabs

PREPARATION TIME: 15 MINUTES + MARINATING
COOKING TIME: 13 MINUTES
SERVES 4
280 CALORIES PER SERVING

---

4 veal escalopes, about 350 g (12 oz) total weight

---

4 slices of Parma ham

---

60 ml (4 tbsp) olive oil

---

30 ml (2 tbsp) white wine vinegar

---

15 ml (1 level tbsp) chopped fresh rosemary

25-50 g (1-2 oz) freshly grated Parmesan cheese

---

lemon wedges, to garnish

---

boiled rice, to serve

---

1 Place the veal escalopes between sheets of greaseproof paper and bat out thinly, using a rolling pin. Cut each escalope into four or five strips.

2 Cut each slice of Parma ham into four or five strips. Place one on each piece of veal and roll up. Place in a non-metallic dish.

3 Mix together the oil, vinegar and rosemary, and pour over the meat rolls. Cover and leave to marinate in the refrigerator for 2 hours.

4 Lift out the veal rolls, reserving the marinade, and thread them on to wooden skewers.

5 Cook the kebabs under a moderate grill for about 12 minutes, turning frequently and basting with the marinade. Sprinkle with the cheese. Grill for 1 minute or until just melted. Serve immediately, garnished with lemon wedges, on a bed of rice.

Parmesan Veal

PREPARATION TIME: 10 MINUTES
COOKING TIME: 20 MINUTES
SERVES 4
360 CALORIES PER SERVING

4 veal escalopes, each weighing about 125 g (4 oz)

salt and pepper

1 egg, beaten

50 g (2 oz) fresh breadcrumbs

60 ml (4 level tbsp) freshly grated Parmesan cheese

30 ml (2 tbsp) olive oil

125 g (4 oz) Italian Mozzarella cheese, sliced

4 tomatoes, sliced

1 Place the veal escalopes between two sheets of greaseproof paper and bat out thinly using a rolling pin. Season with salt and pepper.

2 Pour the egg on to a large plate and mix the breadcrumbs and half of the Parmesan on another plate. Dip the escalopes first into the egg, then into the breadcrumb mixture to coat well.

3 Heat the oil in a large frying pan, add the escalopes and fry for 3-4 minutes on each side or until golden brown.

4 Arrange the escalopes in a shallow ovenproof dish, interleaving them with the Mozzarella and tomato slices. Scatter the remaining Parmesan on top and cook in the oven at 200°C (400°F) mark 6 for 10-15 minutes or until the cheese has melted and the top is beginning to brown. Serve at once.

Basil and Citrus Veal Escalopes

PREPARATION TIME: 10 MINUTES
COOKING TIME: 5 MINUTES
SERVES 4
255 CALORIES PER SERVING

4 veal escalopes
25 g (1 oz) butter
15 ml (1 tbsp) olive oil
100 ml (4 fl oz) orange juice
30 ml (2 tbsp) lemon juice
15 g (½ oz) basil leaves, shredded
salt and pepper
basil sprigs, to garnish

1 Place the veal escalopes between two sheets of greaseproof paper and bat out with a rolling pin until about 3 mm (⅛ inch) thick. If very large, cut them into neat, manageable pieces.

2 Heat the butter and oil in a heavy-based frying pan or sauté pan. Fry the veal, in two batches if necessary, for 1 minute on each side. Add the orange and lemon juices and let bubble for a few seconds, turning the veal in the juice.

3 Add the shredded basil, and season with salt and pepper. Serve immediately, garnished with basil.

COOK'S TIP

For optimum flavour, use freshly squeezed orange juice.

Lamb Cutlets with Apricots

PREPARATION TIME: 10 MINUTES
COOKING TIME: 20 MINUTES
SERVES 4
325 CALORIES PER SERVING

15 g (½ oz) butter

15 ml (1 tbsp) oil

8 lamb cutlets

½ onion, skinned and thinly sliced

75 g (3 oz) no-soak dried apricots, cut into slivers

2.5 ml (½ level tsp) ground cinnamon

150 ml (¼ pint) lamb stock

salt and pepper

1 Heat the butter and oil in a heavy-based frying pan. Add the lamb cutlets and brown on both sides. Remove from the pan and set aside.

2 Add the onion to the pan and cook until softened. Stir in the apricots and cinnamon. Return the lamb cutlets to the pan and pour over the stock. Season with salt and pepper, and bring to the boil, then reduce the heat, cover and simmer gently for 15 minutes or until the meat is tender.

3 Transfer the cutlets to a warmed serving dish and pour the sauce over them.

Spiced Meatballs

PREPARATION TIME: 15 MINUTES + MARINATING
COOKING TIME: 15 MINUTES
MAKES 30 MEATBALLS
70 CALORIES PER MEATBALL

1 large onion, skinned and grated
2 garlic cloves, skinned and crushed
1 green chilli, deseeded and chopped
7.5 ml (1½ level tsp) ground cumin
2.5 ml (½ level tsp) mild chilli seasoning (*not* chilli powder)
450 g (1 lb) minced lamb
2.5 ml (½ level tsp) salt
2.5 ml (½ level tsp) pepper
grated rind and juice of 1 lemon
olive oil
crusty bread, cucumber and feta cheese, to serve
fresh thyme sprigs, to garnish

1 Mix together all the ingredients, except the olive oil, cover and refrigerate overnight.

2 Shape the mixture into small balls, discarding any excess liquid. Brush the grill rack and meatballs lightly with oil.

3 Grill for 10-15 minutes under a high heat, turning frequently. Serve in crusty bread with a cucumber and feta cheese salad. Drizzle over a little warm olive oil with thyme before serving garnished with thyme sprigs.

Sesame Lamb

PREPARATION TIME: **15** MINUTES
COOKING TIME: **15** MINUTES
SERVES **4**
855 CALORIES PER SERVING

2 lamb neck fillets, about 450 g (1 lb) total weight

125 g (4 oz) fresh white breadcrumbs

50 g (2 oz) sesame seeds

salt and pepper

2 eggs, beaten

90 ml (6 tbsp) vegetable oil

1 onion, skinned and sliced lengthways

3 carrots, peeled, sliced and cut into shapes using
small cutters

225 g (8 oz) broccoli, cut into small florets and the stalks cut
diagonally into thin slices

2.5 cm (1 inch) piece of fresh root ginger, peeled and shredded

450 ml (¾ pint) chicken stock

30 ml (2 tbsp) dry sherry

25 ml (1½ level tbsp) cornflour

15 ml (1 tbsp) dark soy sauce

a few drops of sesame oil, to serve

1 Cut the lamb fillets into 5 mm (¼ inch) thick slices. Mix the breadcrumbs with the sesame seeds, and season with salt and pepper.

2 Dip the lamb slices in the beaten egg and coat in the breadcrumb mixture, pressing on firmly with the fingertips.

3 Heat 30 ml (2 tbsp) oil in a wok or large frying pan, add half the lamb slices and fry for about 2 minutes on each side or until golden. Remove from the pan, drain and keep warm. Cook the remaining lamb in the same way, using another 30 ml (2 tbsp) oil.

4   Wipe the pan clean and heat the remaining oil. Add the onion, carrots, broccoli and ginger, and stir-fry for 2 minutes. Add the stock and sherry, cover and steam for 1 minute.

5   Blend the cornflour with the soy sauce and 15 ml (1 tbsp) water, stir into the pan and cook for 2 minutes, stirring. Add the lamb slices and heat through. Sprinkle with sesame oil and serve.

Minted Lamb Escalopes

PREPARATION TIME: 10 MINUTES + MARINATING
COOKING TIME: 6 MINUTES
SERVES 4
210 CALORIES PER SERVING

90 ml (6 level tbsp) Greek natural yogurt
1 garlic clove, skinned and crushed
60 ml (4 level tbsp) chopped fresh mint
30 ml (2 tbsp) lemon juice
salt and 15 ml (1 level tbsp) coarsely ground black pepper
450 g (1 lb) lamb escalopes
mint leaves, to garnish
warm pitta bread and salad, to serve

1 Mix the yogurt, garlic, chopped mint, lemon juice, salt and pepper with the lamb. Place in a non-metallic dish, cover and marinate for 2-3 hours.

2 Grill the lamb for 3 minutes on each side or until golden brown. Garnish with mint and serve immediately with warm pitta bread and salad.

Lamb Fillet and Pepper Stir-fry

PREPARATION TIME: 10 MINUTES
COOKING TIME: ABOUT 10 MINUTES
SERVES 4
275 CALORIES PER SERVING

30 ml (2 tbsp) oil
450 g (1 lb) lamb fillet, thinly sliced
125 g (4 oz) carrots, peeled and sliced diagonally
2 celery sticks, trimmed and thinly sliced
1 red pepper, deseeded and sliced
1 yellow pepper, deseeded and sliced
125 g (4 oz) mangetout
1 large courgette, sliced
45 ml (3 tbsp) garlic and spring onion sauce (see Cook's Tip)
15 ml (1 tbsp) soy sauce
salt and pepper

1 Heat the oil in a large sauté pan or wok and quickly stir-fry the lamb for about 4 minutes, or until almost cooked through and golden brown. Remove from the pan with a slotted spoon and drain on absorbent kitchen paper.

2 Add the carrots, celery and peppers to the pan, and stir-fry for 3-4 minutes.

3 Add all the remaining ingredients, together with the lamb. Cook for a further 2-3 minutes or until the vegetables are just tender. Adjust the seasoning and serve.

COOK'S TIP

Bottled ready-prepared garlic and spring onion sauce is available from large supermarkets and delicatessens. If you do not have any to hand, replace with 30 ml (2 tbsp) sherry and 1 crushed garlic clove.

Roast Lamb Fillet with Garlic and Rosemary

PREPARATION TIME: 10 MINUTES + MARINATING
COOKING TIME: 20 MINUTES
SERVES 6
300 CALORIES PER SERVING

2 large sprigs of fresh rosemary
three 275 g (10 oz) fillets of lamb
45 ml (3 tbsp) olive oil
8-10 garlic cloves, skinned
fresh rosemary, to serve

1 Strip the spiky rosemary leaves off the sprigs. Remove any large pieces of fat from the lamb and put to one side.

2 Place the lamb, olive oil, whole garlic cloves and rosemary in a non-metallic dish, into which they just fit. Cover and leave to marinate overnight in the refrigerator.

3 Place the fat from the lamb in a frying pan and heat gently to extract the oil. Remove and discard the fatty pieces. When the oil in the pan is very hot, remove the lamb and garlic from the marinade and toss quickly in the pan to brown on all sides.

4 Place the lamb fillets and garlic cloves in a roasting tin with the fat from the pan. Spoon over the remaining marinade.

5 Roast in the oven at 200°C (400°F) mark 6 for about 15 minutes for rare meat and about 20 minutes for medium. Serve on a bed of fresh rosemary surrounded by the garlic cloves.

Roast Lamb with a Creamy Fennel Sauce

PREPARATION TIME: 15 MINUTES
COOKING TIME: 30 MINUTES
SERVES 6
365 CALORIES PER SERVING

2 racks of lamb, about 550 g (1¼ lb) each (prepared weight)

salt and pepper

olive oil

700 g (1½ lb) Florence fennel

5 ml (1 level tsp) fennel seeds

40 g (1½ oz) butter

300 ml (½ pint) lamb or beef stock

90 ml (6 level tbsp) double cream

rosemary sprigs, to garnish (optional)

1 Trim the lamb of any excess fat and divide each rack into three. Season the lamb with salt and pepper, and place in a roasting tin. Drizzle with olive oil.

2 Roast the lamb in the oven at 200°C (400°F) mark 6 for about 25 minutes for medium rare, about 30 minutes for well done.

3 Meanwhile, finely slice the fennel, discarding the core and reserving the feathery tops. Crush the fennel seeds with the end of a rolling pin.

4 Melt the butter in a frying pan, add the fennel and fennel seeds, and fry gently, stirring, for about 10 minutes or until the fennel has softened. Add the stock and bring to the boil, then reduce the heat and simmer gently for 2 minutes. Stir in the cream and simmer until beginning to thicken.

5 Serve the sauce with the lamb. Chop the reserved fennel tops and sprinkle over the lamb and sauce. Garnish with rosemary sprigs, if wished.

Satay-style Pork

PREPARATION TIME: 20 MINUTES
COOKING TIME: 10 MINUTES
SERVES 4
250 CALORIES PER SERVING

450 g (1 lb) pork fillet, cubed

90 ml (6 level tbsp) Greek natural yogurt

90 ml (6 level tbsp) bottled satay marinade

15 ml (1 tbsp) lemon juice

5 ml (1 level tsp) ground cumin

15 ml (1 tbsp) oil

salt and pepper

lemon slices and mint, to garnish

1 Place the pork in a bowl, add the next five ingredients, and season with salt and pepper. Stir well until the meat is evenly coated, then cover and refrigerate for at least 15 minutes.

2 Thread the meat on to four skewers and brush with the marinade. Place under a preheated grill for about 10 minutes or until cooked through, basting with some of the marinade and turning occasionally.

3 Place the remaining marinade in a small saucepan and heat very gently, taking care not to boil. Pour over the meat and serve.

Pork with Glazed Aubergine

PREPARATION TIME: 10 MINUTES
COOKING TIME: 15 MINUTES
SERVES 4
430 CALORIES PER SERVING

4 rindless pork chops, about 175 g (6 oz) each

2 garlic cloves, skinned and sliced

150 g (5 oz) jar of teriyaki sauce

1 large aubergine, about 350 g (12 oz)

1 large Spanish onion, about 225 g (8 oz), skinned

60 ml (4 tbsp) oil

150 ml (¼ pint) unsweetened orange juice or the juice of
2 large oranges

1 Trim the pork chops of excess fat, then pierce all over with the point of a sharp knife. Insert the garlic slices into the cuts. Place the chops on a foil-lined grill pan and brush one side lightly with teriyaki sauce - you'll need 15-30 ml (1-2 tbsp). Grill for about 7 minutes, then turn the chops over, brush with a little more teriyaki sauce and grill for a further 7 minutes or until tender and well glazed.

2 Meanwhile, dice the aubergine and roughly chop the onion. Fry in the oil for 8-10 minutes, stirring occasionally, until golden brown.

3 Stir the remaining teriyaki sauce and the orange juice into the aubergine mixture. Bring to the boil and bubble for 1-2 minutes. Serve with the pork.

Pork with Spiced Butter

PREPARATION TIME: 5 MINUTES
COOKING TIME: 20 MINUTES
SERVES 4
455 CALORIES PER SERVING

---

300 ml (½ pint) cider

---

30 ml (2 level tbsp) mixed peppercorns

---

60 ml (4 level tbsp) brown sugar

---

60 ml (4 level tbsp) wholegrain mustard

---

50 g (2 oz) butter

---

salt and pepper

---

4 pork chops, about 175 g (6 oz) each

---

1 Put the cider in a small saucepan and boil for 15 minutes.

2 Meanwhile, crush the peppercorns, then combine with the sugar, mustard and butter.

3 Season the chops with salt and pepper, and cook under a preheated grill for 5 minutes on one side. Turn over, spread each chop with the flavoured butter, then cook for a further 5 minutes or until golden and cooked through.

4 Pour the grill pan juices into the cider and heat for 2-3 minutes. Pour over the pork chops and serve.

Stir-fried Pork and Vegetables

PREPARATION TIME: 15 MINUTES
COOKING TIME: 10 MINUTES
SERVES 4
395 CALORIES PER SERVING

700 g (1½ lb) pork fillet, trimmed and cut into thin strips

60 ml (4 tbsp) dry sherry

45 ml (3 tbsp) dark soy sauce

10 ml (2 level tsp) ground ginger

salt and pepper

1 cucumber

30 ml (2 tbsp) oil

1 bunch of spring onions, trimmed and finely chopped

1-2 garlic cloves, skinned and crushed (optional)

30 ml (2 level tbsp) cornflour

300 ml (½ pint) cold chicken stock

175 g (6 oz) beansprouts

1 Put the pork strips in a bowl with the sherry, soy sauce and ginger. Season with salt and pepper, stir well to mix, and set aside.

2 Cut the cucumber in half, then cut it lengthways into quarters, discarding the rounded ends. Leave the skin on, to add colour.

3 Using a sharp-edged teaspoon, scoop out the cucumber seeds and discard. Cut each cucumber piece lengthways in half again, then slice across into strips about 2.5 cm (1 inch) long.

4 Heat the oil in a wok or large frying pan, add the spring onions and garlic, if using, and fry gently for about 5 minutes or until softened.

5 Add the pork to the pan, increase the heat and stir-fry for 2-3 minutes or until lightly coloured. Mix the cornflour with the chicken stock and set aside.

6 Add the cucumber and beansprouts to the pork, with the cornflour and stock. Stir-fry until the juices thicken and the ingredients are well combined. Turn into a warmed serving dish and serve immediately.

Pork with Italian Salsa

PREPARATION TIME: 5 MINUTES
COOKING TIME: 10 MINUTES
SERVES 4
470 CALORIES PER SERVING

30 ml (2 level tbsp) capers, roughly chopped

25 g (1 oz) pitted black or green olives, roughly chopped

50 g (2 oz) sun-dried tomatoes, roughly chopped

50 g (2 oz) can of anchovy fillets, roughly chopped

juice of 2 lemons

4 garlic cloves, skinned and crushed

75 ml (3 fl oz) olive oil

60 ml (4 level tbsp) chopped fresh parsley

salt and pepper

4 pork chops, about 175 g (6 oz) each

fresh basil, to garnish

1 To make the salsa, mix together all the ingredients, except the chops.

2 Pan-fry or grill the chops for about 5 minutes on each side. Serve with the salsa and sprigs of basil.

Pork Kebabs

Preparation time: 10 minutes + marinating
Cooking time: 12-15 minutes
Serves 4
480 calories per serving

900 g (2 lb) lean pork, cut into 2.5 cm (1 inch) cubes
60 ml (4 tbsp) olive oil
5 ml (1 level tsp) ground cumin
5 ml (1 level tsp) paprika
30 ml (2 level tbsp) chopped fresh oregano or thyme
1 small onion, skinned and very finely chopped
1 lemon
salt and pepper
8 bay leaves

1 Put the pork in a large, non-metallic dish. Mix together the oil, cumin, paprika, oregano and onion. Grate the rind from half the lemon, then cut the lemon in half. Squeeze the juice from the grated half and cut the remaining half into eight wedges.

2 Add the lemon rind and juice to the oil mixture and season with salt and pepper. Pour the marinade over the pork, mix well, cover and leave to marinate in the refrigerator for several hours or overnight, stirring occasionally.

3 Thread the pork, lemon wedges and bay leaves alternately on to four long skewers. Place the kebabs on an oiled grill rack and grill under a hot grill for 12-15 minutes, turning frequently, until the pork is cooked and browned.

VARIATION

Use lean lamb (from the shoulder or leg) instead of pork for a delicious variation, and flavour the marinade with mint instead of oregano or thyme.

Pork Medallions in Creamy Sloe-Gin Sauce

PREPARATION TIME: 5 MINUTES
COOKING TIME: 25-30 MINUTES
SERVES 6
595 CALORIES PER SERVING

900 g (2 lb) pork fillet

30 ml (2 tbsp) olive oil

50 g (2 oz) butter

300 ml (½ pint) sloe gin (see Cook's Tip)

300 ml (½ pint) beef stock

75 g (3 oz) raisins

142 ml (5 fl oz) carton of double cream

salt and pepper

1 Trim the pork fillet and cut into 1 cm (½ inch) thick slices. Heat the oil and butter in a large sauté pan, add the pork in batches, and fry until browned. Drain on absorbent kitchen paper.

2 Add the sloe gin, stock and raisins to the pan, then bring to a gentle simmer, scraping up any caramelised sediment from the base of the pan. Return the pork to the pan, cover and simmer gently for 10-15 minutes or until tender.

3 Lift the pork out of the sauce and transfer to a warm serving dish. Cover and keep warm in a low oven. Bring the sauce to the boil and boil rapidly for about 2 minutes to reduce slightly. Add the cream and continue to bubble for a further 2 minutes or until the sauce becomes syrupy, stirring occasionally. Season and pour over the pork. Serve immediately.

COOK'S TIP

Sloe gin is available in large supermarkets and good off-licences, but if you can't find it, use 150 ml (¼ pint) gin with an extra 150 ml (¼ pint) stock and 30 ml (2 level tbsp) redcurrant jelly in its place.

Mushroom and Ham Risotto

PREPARATION TIME: 5 MINUTES
COOKING TIME: 25 MINUTES
SERVES 4
445 CALORIES PER SERVING

---

50 g (2 oz) butter

---

125 g (4 oz) onion, skinned and finely chopped

---

1 bay leaf

---

2 garlic cloves, skinned

---

pinch of saffron strands

---

225 g (8 oz) Arborio (risotto) rice

---

150 ml (¼ pint) dry white wine

---

750 ml (1¼ pints) chicken stock

---

15 g (½ oz) dried porcini mushrooms or 285 g (10 oz) jar of
funghi tripolati antipasto, drained

---

salt and pepper

---

350 g (12 oz) cooked ham, cut into bite-sized pieces

---

pared Cheddar cheese, to garnish

---

1 Melt the butter in a large saucepan. Add the onion, bay leaf and whole garlic, and fry, stirring, for 4-5 minutes or until the onion is soft but not coloured.

2 Stir in the remaining ingredients, except the ham. Bring to the boil, then reduce the heat and simmer gently for 15 minutes.

3 Add the ham and continue cooking for 5 minutes or until most of the liquid has been absorbed and rice is tender, stirring frequently. Add a little more stock if necessary. Adjust the seasoning and garnish with cheese.

Calf's Liver with Grapes and Madeira

PREPARATION TIME: 5 MINUTES
COOKING TIME: 10 MINUTES
SERVES 4
330 CALORIES PER SERVING

50 g (2 oz) butter or margarine
50 g (2 oz) onion or shallot, skinned and finely chopped
175 ml (6 fl oz) veal or chicken stock
100 ml (4 fl oz) Madeira
salt and pepper
24 large green grapes, peeled, halved and deseeded
4 slices of calf's liver, each about 75-100 g (3-4 oz)
4 sage leaves, thinly sliced
sage sprigs, to garnish

1 Melt half the butter in a frying pan and fry the onion until golden. Add the stock and Madeira, season with salt and pepper, and bring to the boil. Boil rapidly for 4-5 minutes or until reduced to a slightly syrupy consistency. Add the grape halves and warm through gently.

2 Meanwhile, melt the remaining butter in a large frying pan. Season the liver and fry, with the sliced sage leaves, for 3-5 minutes, turning once.

3 Remove the liver from the pan and serve at once, with the Madeira sauce. Garnish with sage sprigs.

Kidneys in Sherry Sauce

PREPARATION TIME: 10 MINUTES
COOKING TIME: 20 MINUTES
SERVES 4
430 CALORIES PER SERVING

16 lamb's kidneys, about 900 g (2 lb) total weight

salt and pepper

30 ml (2 tbsp) olive oil

2 onions, skinned and finely chopped

2 garlic cloves, skinned and crushed

30 ml (2 level tbsp) chopped fresh parsley

45 ml (3 level tbsp) plain flour

350 ml (12 fl oz) dry sherry

350 ml (12 fl oz) beef stock

chopped fresh parsley, to garnish

1 Cut the kidneys in half. Remove the cores and fat, then cut each in half again. Sprinkle with salt and pepper.

2 Heat the oil in a large frying pan and fry the kidneys over a high heat for 1 minute. Transfer to a warm dish. Add the onion, garlic and parsley to the pan, and fry gently until soft. Stir in the flour and cook for 1 minute. Add the sherry and stock, stirring continuously, and cook, stirring, until thickened and smooth. Cover and simmer gently for 10 minutes.

3 Return the kidneys to the pan and simmer for a further 5-10 minutes. Serve hot, garnished with chopped parsley.

COOK'S TIPS

Be careful not to overcook the kidneys or they will become tough. The insides should be just pale pink. If you prefer a smooth sauce, sieve the sauce before returning the kidneys to the pan in step 3.

Gammon with Crunchy Nut Glaze

PREPARATION TIME: 10 MINUTES
COOKING TIME: 15 MINUTES
SERVES 8
390 CALORIES PER SERVING

60 ml (4 tbsp) runny honey

15 ml (1 level tbsp) Dijon mustard

1.6-1.8 kg (3½-4 lb) precooked corner gammon joint (see Cook's Tip)

about 10 cloves

30 ml (2 level tbsp) sesame seeds

15 ml (1 level tbsp) white mustard seeds

15 ml (1 level tbsp) white mustard seeds

25 g (1 oz) flaked almonds

pickled pears, to garnish (optional)

1 Mix together the honey and Dijon mustard

2 With a sharp knife, carefully strip the rind from the cooked gammon joint and score the fat. Place in a roasting tin. Press the cloves into the scored fat and brush with half the honey and mustard glaze.

3 Add the sesame seeds, mustard seeds and almonds tohe glaze and press on to the fat. Cook in the oven at 200°C (400°F) mark 6 for about 15 minutes. Serve hot or cold, carved into slices, with pickled peqars, if desired.

COOK'S TIP

If you prefer to cook the gammon at home rather than buying it precooked, place the joint in a roasting tin on a bed of bay leaves. Season well with black pepper. Add 300 ml (1/2 pint) water and cover with foil. Cook in the oven at 180°C (350°F) mark 4 for 20 minutes per 450 g (1 lb), turning the gammon over once during cooking. Continue as above.

Quick Stir-fry Ideas

*For a quick supper for two, stir-fry 300 g (10 oz) of pork,
lamb or beef cut into strips across the grain, with one of the
following combinations:*

✦ 2 medium shredded leeks, 125 g (4 oz) chestnut mushrooms, a handful of beansprouts and 15 ml (1 level tbsp) of mustard seeds. Season with 30 ml (2 tbsp) light soy sauce and a large pinch of freshly grated ginger.

✦ 1-2 garlic cloves, 1-2 chopped chillies, 1 large can of drained canned pimientos, and lots of chopped fresh coriander.

✦ 3 large shredded courgettes and half a bunch of spring onions. Season with 15 ml (1 tbsp) each of honey, wholegrain mustard and orange juice. Add lots of chopped watercress off the heat.

✦ 225 g (8 oz) par-boiled baby potatoes, 225 g (8 oz) onion quarters, 125 g (4 oz) green beans. Season with a crushed clove of garlic and 10 ml (2 tsp) bottled curry paste. Stir through 150 ml (¼ pint) thick yogurt just before serving.

✦ 225 g (8 oz) sugar snap peas or mangetout and 15-30 ml (1-2 tbsp) bottled Thai green curry paste. Moisten with 150 ml (¼ pint) coconut milk.

✦ Half a can of sliced bamboo shoots and 3 carrots, and a handful of shredded Chinese leaves. Flavour with 30 ml (2 tbsp) bottled hoisin sauce and a large pinch of Chinese five-spice powder.

✦ 175 g (6 oz) okra, 2 medium sliced onions and one large sliced red pepper.

✦ 2 small sliced courgettes, 1 small aubergine cut into strips, 6 artichoke hearts and 2 chopped fresh tomatoes. Flavour with a crushed clove of garlic, 15 ml (1 tbsp) capers, a handful of flat-leaf parsley and 5 ml (1 level tsp) grated lemon rind.

✦ 125 g (4 oz) egg noodles, a splash of sesame oil, 30 ml (2 tbsp) sesame seeds and 225 g (8 oz) of your favourite vegetables cut into strips.

Poultry

Glazed Cashew Nut Chicken

PREPARATION TIME: 10 MINUTES
COOKING TIME: 10 MINUTES
SERVES 4
335 CALORIES PER SERVING

15 ml (1 tbsp) oil

1 red pepper, deseeded and sliced

450 g (1 lb) skinless chicken breast fillet, cut into strips

3 garlic cloves, skinned and crushed

30 ml (2 tbsp) Thai-style fish sauce

30 ml (2 tbsp) oyster sauce

30 ml (2 level tbsp) soft brown sugar

75 g (3 oz) toasted cashew nuts

4 spring onions, green tips only, roughly chopped

1 Heat the oil in a wok or frying pan and fry the pepper, chicken and garlic over a high heat for about 2 minutes. Add the fish sauce, oyster sauce and sugar, and continue to cook, stirring, until the chicken is tender and all the ingredients are evenly glazed.

2 Stir in the cashew nuts and chopped spring onion tips. Serve immediately.

Red Hot Jungle Curry

PREPARATION TIME: 10 MINUTES
COOKING TIME: 15 MINUTES
SERVES 4
200 CALORIES PER SERVING

15 ml (1 tbsp) oil

350 g (12 oz) skinless chicken breast fillet, cut into strips

30 ml (2 level tbsp) red curry paste

125 g (4 oz) aubergine, cut into bite-sized pieces

125 g (4 oz) baby sweetcorn, halved lengthways

75 g (3 oz) green beans, topped and tailed

75 g (3 oz) button or brown-cap mushrooms, wiped and
halved if necessary

2-3 Kaffir lime leaves (optional, see page 55)

2.5 cm (1 inch) piece of fresh root ginger, peeled and finely
sliced

450 ml (¾ pint) chicken stock

30 ml (2 tbsp) Thai-style fish sauce

grated rind of ½ lime

5 ml (1 level tsp) tomato purée

15 ml (1 level tbsp) soft brown sugar

pared lime rind, to garnish

1 Heat the oil in a wok or large frying pan. Add the chicken and cook, stirring, for 5 minutes or until the chicken turns golden brown.

2 Add the red curry paste and cook for a further minute. Add the vegetables and lime leaves, if using, and stir until coated in the red curry paste. Add all the remaining ingredients and bring to the boil. Reduce the heat and simmer gently for 10-12 minutes or until the chicken and vegetables are just tender. Serve immediately, garnished with pared lime rind.

Chicken in Smoky Bacon Sauce

PREPARATION TIME: 10 MINUTES
COOKING TIME: 20 MINUTES
SERVES 4
350 CALORIES PER SERVING

---

30 ml (2 tbsp) oil

---

125 g (4 oz) chopped bacon pieces or thin-cut, smoked, streaky bacon, roughly chopped

---

4 skinless chicken supremes or breast fillets, about 150 g (5 oz) each

---

200 ml (7 fl oz) carton of apple juice

---

15 ml (1 level tbsp) chopped fresh thyme or 5 ml (1 level tsp) dried thyme

---

salt and pepper

---

1 bunch of spring onions, trimmed and chopped

---

225 g (8 oz) crisp red apples, cored and thickly sliced

---

60 ml (4 level tbsp) crème fraîche

---

noodles or pasta, to serve

---

1 Heat the oil in a large, deep frying pan or sauté pan, preferably non-stick. Add the bacon and chicken supremes, and fry for a few minutes or until golden, stirring and turning occasionally.

2 Stir in the apple juice and thyme, and season with salt and pepper. Bring to the boil, then reduce the heat, cover and simmer for 10 minutes.

3 Uncover, then add the spring onions. Add the apples to the pan and cook over a high heat for about 5 minutes or until the liquid has reduced by half and the chicken is tender.

4 Over a low heat, stir in the crème fraîche. Adjust the seasoning and serve with noodles.

Grilled Coriander and Lime Chicken

PREPARATION TIME: 5 MINUTES
COOKING TIME: ABOUT 25 MINUTES
SERVES 4
435 CALORIES PER SERVING

grated rind and juice of 2 limes

75 ml (5 level tbsp) chopped fresh coriander

2 garlic cloves, skinned and crushed

30 ml (2 tbsp) dry vermouth

50 ml (2 fl oz) olive oil

10 ml (2 tsp) runny honey

salt and pepper

4 chicken breast fillets with skin, 175 g (6 oz) each

5 spring onions or a small bunch of chives

halved limes, to garnish

1 Mix together the grated rind and juice of the whole limes with 45 ml (3 level tbsp) chopped fresh coriander, the garlic, vermouth, olive oil, honey and plenty of salt and pepper.

2 Coat the chicken breasts with the lime mixture. Line a grill pan with foil and grill the chicken breasts for 10-12 minutes on each side, basting with the marinade, until they are cooked through and golden brown.

3 Meanwhile, roughly chop the spring onions or chives diagonally. Toss with the remaining chopped coriander.

4 To serve, spoon any remaining pan juices over the fillets and sprinkle with spring onions or chives and chopped coriander. Garnish and serve.

Stir-fried Chicken with Courgettes

PREPARATION TIME: 10 MINUTES
COOKING TIME: 7-10 MINUTES
SERVES 4
250 CALORIES PER SERVING

450 g (1 lb) courgettes

1 red pepper

450 g (1 lb) skinless chicken breast fillets

30 ml (2 tbsp) oil

1 garlic clove, skinned and crushed

45 ml (3 tbsp) dry sherry

15 ml (1 tbsp) light soy sauce

pepper

boiled rice or noodles, to serve

1 Cut the courgettes into long thin strips. Cut the pepper into strips, discarding the core and seeds.

2 Slice the chicken into thin strips. Heat the oil in a wok or large frying pan, and fry the garlic for 1 minute. Add the chicken and cook for 3-4 minutes, stirring continuously.

3 Add the courgettes and pepper, and continue to cook for 1-2 minutes or until the chicken is cooked and the vegetables are tender but still crisp. Stir in the sherry and soy sauce and cook for 1 minute. Season with pepper. Serve immediately, with boiled rice or noodles.

Chicken and Gorgonzola Parcels

PREPARATION TIME: 5 MINUTES
COOKING TIME: 25 MINUTES
SERVES 4
450 CALORIES PER SERVING

4 skinless chicken breast fillets, about 700 g (1½ lb)
total weight

10 ml (2 level tsp) olive paste or finely chopped, black,
pitted olives

125 g (4 oz) Gorgonzola (or Dolcelatte, St Agur,
or Stilton), sliced

12 fresh sage leaves

4 slices of Parma ham or prosciutto crudo

25 g (1 oz) butter

75 g (3 oz) shallots, skinned and finely chopped

150 ml (¼ pint) dry vermouth or white wine

salt and pepper

crisp green vegetables and new potatoes, to serve

1 Starting at the thick side, cut a deep horizontal pocket in each chicken breast. Spread a little olive paste inside each pocket, then stuff with the cheese. Lay three sage leaves on top of each breast. Wrap each breast in a slice of Parma ham, tying with fine string.

2 Heat the butter in a sauté pan or heavy frying pan and cook the shallots for 5 minutes or until beginning to soften. Place the chicken on top of the shallots and pour in the vermouth or wine. Bring to the boil, then reduce the heat, cover and simmer for about 20 minutes or until the chicken is tender and cooked through. Season the sauce with salt and pepper.

3 Remove the string from the chicken. Serve immediately with a little sauce poured over, accompanied by crisp green vegetables and new potatoes.

Cajun Spiced Chicken

PREPARATION TIME: 10 MINUTES
COOKING TIME: 15 MINUTES
SERVES 6
180 CALORIES PER SERVING

This Cajun-style seasoning can be used for spicing up fish too.

10 ml (2 level tsp) each paprika, dried thyme, oregano and rock salt
5 ml (1 level tsp) each ground black pepper, mustard powder and cayenne pepper
6 chicken supremes
15 ml (1 tbsp) olive oil
4 limes

1 Mix together the herbs, spices and seasoning. Brush the chicken with olive oil and sprinkle with the spice mixture, pressing it on to the skin with your hands if necessary. Slice 1 lime and halve the remainder.

2 Thread a slice of lime on to each of six large metal or bamboo skewers followed by a chicken supreme.

3 Barbecue or grill for 10-15 minutes or until golden and cooked through, turning once during cooking. Alternatively, place the chicken with some lime slices in a roasting tin and cook in the oven at 200°C (400°F) mark 6 for 25-30 minutes. Serve with lime halves.

Chicken Breasts with Mustard and Parma Ham

PREPARATION TIME: 5 MINUTES
COOKING TIME: 30 MINUTES
SERVES 4
175 CALORIES PER SERVING

75 g (3 oz) reduced-fat soft cheese

15 ml (1 level tbsp) wholegrain mustard

4 skinless chicken breast fillets, about 75 g (3 oz) each

8 slices of Parma ham or thin slices of cooked ham

1 Mix together the soft cheese and mustard. Using a sharp knife, make a lengthways slit in each chicken breast, and pile the cheese mixture into the slit.

2 Wrap each chicken breast in two slices of ham and enclose in a foil parcel. Place in a baking tin and cook in the oven at 190°C (375°F) mark 5 for 30 minutes or until the chicken is cooked.

VARIATIONS

Omit the mustard and add 25 g (1 oz) chopped sun-dried tomatoes and 25 g (1 oz) chopped black olives to the soft cheese. (Adds an extra 30 calories per serving.)

Heat 15 g (½ oz) butter in a non-stick pan and cook 275 g (10 oz) sliced mushrooms, 1 crushed garlic clove and 10 ml (2 tsp) lemon juice until all the liquid has evaporated. Cool, then put in a food processor with 75 g (3 oz) reduced-fat soft cheese. Blend until smooth, then use to stuff the chicken breasts, wrap with ham and cook as above. (Adds an extra 40 calories per serving.)

Omit the mustard and add 1 crushed garlic clove and about 45 ml (3 level tbsp) chopped fresh herbs to the cheese.

Pan-fried Chicken with Yellow Peppers and Carrot

PREPARATION TIME: 10 MINUTES
COOKING TIME: 20-25 MINUTES
SERVES 4
355 CALORIES PER SERVING

---

4 skinless chicken breast fillets

---

45 ml (3 tbsp) olive oil

½ onion, skinned and finely sliced

---

2 garlic cloves, skinned and crushed

---

2 yellow peppers, deseeded and sliced

---

2 carrots, peeled and cut into matchsticks

---

2 celery sticks, sliced diagonally

---

4 plum tomatoes, quartered

---

salt and pepper

---

150 ml (¼ pint) dry white wine

---

1 Slash each chicken breast two or three times with a sharp knife. Heat the oil in a large frying pan, add the chicken and fry for 5-8 minutes, turning frequently, until evenly browned. Add the onion, garlic, peppers, carrots, celery and tomatoes. Season, then cover the pan and cook for 5 minutes.

2 Pour in the wine and cook over moderate heat for 10-15 minutes or until the chicken is tender and the juices are reduced. Adjust the seasoning and serve hot.

Creamy Chicken Gratin

PREPARATION TIME: 10 MINUTES
COOKING TIME: 20 MINUTES
SERVES 4
840 CALORIES PER SERVING

350 g (12 oz) trimmed leeks
225 g (8 oz) cooked chicken, skinned
125 g (4 oz) rindless streaky bacon
225 g (8 oz) Gruyère cheese
1 small baguette
75 g (3 oz) garlic butter
30 ml (2 level tbsp) plain flour
300 ml (½ pint) milk
30 ml (2 level tbsp) chopped fresh parsley

1 Cut the leeks, chicken and bacon into chunks. Grate or crumble the cheese. Slice the baguette into about 16 slices. Using half of the prepared garlic butter, spread each slice of the French bread on one side only.

2 Fry the bacon in a large non-stick saucepan for about 5 minutes or until golden and crispy, then lift out with a slotted spoon. Melt the remaining garlic butter together with the bacon fat and use to sauté the leeks for about 7 minutes or until soft but not coloured.

3 Add the flour, stir well, then gradually add the milk and bring to the boil. Reduce the heat and simmer for about 5 minutes or until the sauce has thickened. Over a low heat, add the chicken and simmer gently, stirring, for about 3 minutes or until the chicken is hot. Stir in all but 50 g (2 oz) of the cheese.

4 Stir the bacon and parsley into the sauce. Pour into a shallow ovenproof dish and top with the slices of bread, butter side uppermost, and the remaining cheese. Place under a hot grill for about 5 minutes or until the cheese is golden brown and bubbling.

Warm Chicken and Wheat Salad

PREPARATION TIME: 20 MINUTES + MARINATING
COOKING TIME: 10 MINUTES
SERVES 4
340 CALORIES PER SERVING

350 g (12 oz) skinless chicken breast fillet

30 ml (2 level tbsp) mango chutney

45 ml (3 tbsp) lemon or lime juice

30 ml (2 tbsp) oil

10 ml (2 level tsp) garam masala or mild curry powder

5 ml (1 level tsp) paprika

salt and pepper

125 g (4 oz) bulghur wheat

1 cucumber

1 bunch of spring onions, trimmed and thinly sliced

25 g (1 oz) no-soak dried apricots, thinly sliced

30 ml (2 level tbsp) chopped fresh mint

60 ml (4 level tbsp) low-fat natural yogurt and shredded fresh
mint leaves, to serve

1 Cut the chicken into thick strips. In a bowl, mix together the next five ingredients and season well with salt and pepper. Stir in the chicken. Cover and refrigerate for at least 1 hour, preferably overnight.

2 Place the bulghur wheat in a bowl, pour over 200 ml (7 fl oz) boiling water and leave to soak for about 30 minutes or until all the liquid has been absorbed. (Follow the packet instructions as some bulghur wheat takes longer to soften.) Meanwhile, cut the cucumber lengthways into quarters and remove the seeds. Roughly chop the cucumber, place in a nylon sieve, sprinkle with salt and leave for about 30 minutes. Rinse and drain well.

3 Mix the bulghur wheat with the cucumber, spring onions, apricots, chopped mint and seasoning. Spoon on to a serving dish.

4 Gently warm a non-stick frying pan over a moderate heat. Add the chicken and marinade and cook over a high heat for 2-3 minutes, stirring frequently. Pour in 150 ml (¼ pint) water. Bring to the boil and cook, uncovered, for about 5 minutes or until the chicken is tender and the sauce reduced.

5 Spoon the warm chicken and sauce on to the bulghur wheat salad and serve with natural yogurt, mixed with a few shredded mint leaves.

Quick Coronation Salad

PREPARATION TIME: 10 MINUTES
SERVES 4
240 CALORIES PER SERVING

142 ml (5 fl oz) carton of low-fat natural yogurt
60 ml (4 level tbsp) reduced-calorie mayonnaise
30 ml (2 level tbsp) mild curry paste
10 ml (2 tsp) runny honey
350 g (12 oz) skinless cooked chicken, shredded
225 g (8 oz) celery, trimmed and sliced
125 g (4 oz) seedless grapes, halved
1 eating apple, cored and chopped
salt and pepper
crisp salad leaves, to serve

1 In a large bowl, mix the yogurt and mayonnaise together and stir in the curry paste and honey.

2 Add the chicken, celery, grapes and apple to the yogurt mixture. Season with salt and pepper and mix well. Serve on a bed of salad leaves.

Chicken Koftas with Mint Dip

PREPARATION TIME: 20 MINUTES
COOKING TIME: 6-8 MINUTES
SERVES 8
175 CALORIES PER SERVING

225 g (8 oz) cooked chicken meat, skinned

50 g (2 oz) white bread, crusts removed

1 egg, lightly beaten

10 ml (2 tsp) lemon juice

a little freshly grated nutmeg

salt and pepper

flour, for coating

oil for deep-frying

For the dip

225 ml (8 fl oz) Greek natural yogurt

60 ml (4 level tbsp) chopped fresh mint

10 ml (2 tsp) mint jelly

salt and pepper

fresh mint leaves and cucumber slices, to garnish

1 Mince the chicken finely and set aside. Soak the bread in 45 ml (3 tbsp) water for 5 minutes, then squeeze dry with your hands.

2 Mix the bread with the chicken, egg, lemon juice and nutmeg. Season with salt and pepper. Continue mixing for a few minutes or until all the ingredients are well blended. Shape the mixture into 32 tiny balls and toss lightly in flour.

3 To make the dip, put the yogurt, chopped mint and mint jelly in a blender or food processor and process until evenly blended. Season with salt and pepper.

4 Heat the oil in a deep-fat fryer to 180°C (350°F) or until a 2.5 cm (1 inch) cube of bread browns in the hot oil in 45 seconds. Fry the koftas, in two batches, for 3-4 minutes or until golden brown. Drain well on absorbent kitchen paper. Serve warm or cold, and garnish the mint dip with mint leaves and cucumber slices.

Grilled Chicken with Salsa Verde

PREPARATION TIME: 15 MINUTES
COOKING TIME: 12-16 MINUTES
SERVES 6
385 CALORIES PER SERVING

3 anchovy fillets in oil, drained
2 garlic cloves, skinned and crushed
2.5 ml (½ tsp) balsamic or sherry vinegar
15 ml (1 level tbsp) capers, chopped
60 ml (4 level tbsp) chopped fresh parsley
150 ml (¼ pint) olive oil
pepper
6 chicken breast fillets, about 175 g (6 oz) each

1 Pound the anchovies in a pestle and mortar or in a strong bowl with the end of a rolling pin. Stir in the garlic and vinegar.

2 Beat in the capers and parsley, gradually adding the olive oil. Season with pepper. (You should not need to add salt as the anchovies are salty enough.)

3 Cook the chicken breasts under a moderate grill for 6-8 minutes on each side, or until they are cooked through. Serve each with a few spoonfuls of the salsa.

Braised Chicken with Peppers

PREPARATION TIME: 15 MINUTES + MARINATING
COOKING TIME: 16 MINUTES
SERVES 4
360 CALORIES PER SERVING

450 g (1 lb) skinless chicken breast fillets, cut into bite-sized pieces

15 ml (1 tbsp) dark soy sauce

30 ml (2 tbsp) light soy sauce

30 ml (2 tbsp) dry sherry

30 ml (2 level tbsp) sugar

1 garlic clove, skinned and crushed

salt and pepper

45 ml (3 tbsp) oil

1 large onion, skinned and cut into very thin slivers

1 large red pepper, deseeded and cut into thin slivers

1 large green pepper, deseeded and cut into thin slivers

175 ml (6 fl oz) chicken stock

30 ml (2 level tbsp) cornflour

60 ml (4 tbsp) dry white wine

16 canned water chestnuts, sliced

1 Put the chicken pieces in a bowl. Add the soy sauces, sherry, sugar and garlic, and season. Cover and leave to marinate for 30 minutes.

2 Heat the oil in a wok or large frying pan, add the onion and peppers, and stir-fry for 2 minutes. Remove from the pan and reserve.

3 Add the chicken mixture and stock to the pan and bring to the boil, then reduce the heat, cover and simmer for 10 minutes, stirring occasionally.

4 Blend the cornflour with 30 ml (2 tbsp) water and the wine. Add this mixture to the pan and cook for 2 minutes, stirring.

5 Stir in the onion and peppers with the water chestnuts and heat through for about 2 minutes, stirring frequently. Serve hot.

Thai Grilled Chicken

PREPARATION TIME: 10 MINUTES + MARINATING
COOKING TIME: 12 MINUTES
SERVES 4
270 CALORIES PER SERVING

1 medium red chilli, deseeded
2 garlic cloves, skinned
5 spring onions, trimmed and roughly chopped
10 ml (2 level tsp) sugar
125 g (4 oz) creamed coconut, roughly chopped
10 ml (2 tsp) Thai-style fish sauce
15 ml (1 level tbsp) chopped fresh coriander
4 skinless chicken breast fillets, about 125 g (4 oz) each

1 Put all the ingredients, except the chicken, in a food processor with 150 ml (¼ pint) warm water. Blend until almost smooth.

2 Cut four slashes in each chicken breast, then place in a non-metallic dish and spoon the marinade over. Turn to coat, then cover and leave to marinate for 1 hour.

3 Place the chicken on a foil-lined grill pan with half the marinade. Grill for 6 minutes on each side (spread the remaining marinade over the second side) or until cooked.

Oriental Chicken

PREPARATION TIME: 15 MINUTES + MARINATING
COOKING TIME: ABOUT 20 MINUTES
SERVES 4
305 CALORIES PER SERVING

2.5 cm (1 inch) piece of fresh root ginger, peeled and finely chopped

1 large garlic clove, skinned and crushed

200 ml (7 fl oz) orange juice

60 ml (4 tbsp) lemon juice

60 ml (4 tbsp) light soy sauce

60 ml (4 tbsp) sherry

15 ml (1 tbsp) white wine vinegar

5 ml (1 level tsp) runny honey

4 skinless chicken breast fillets, about 450 g (1 lb) total weight

175 g (6 oz) baby sweetcorn, halved lengthways

salt and pepper

125 g (4 oz) beansprouts

15 ml (1 tbsp) sunflower oil

1 small head of Chinese leaves, shredded

1 head of radicchio lettuce, shredded

1 bunch of spring onions, trimmed and sliced

15 ml (1 level tbsp) sesame seeds, toasted, to garnish

1 Mix together the first eight ingredients and place in a large, shallow, non-metallic dish.

2 Make three shallow cuts in each chicken breast and place in the marinade. Cover and chill for 3-4 hours (the longer the better).

3 Cook the sweetcorn in boiling salted water for about 5 minutes. Add the beansprouts and cook for 30 seconds. Drain, dry with absorbent kitchen paper and leave to cool.

4 Remove the chicken from the marinade. Heat the oil in a large non-stick pan and cook the chicken for 10-12 minutes, turning frequently, until cooked through. Add the marinade to the pan and simmer to thicken slightly. Adjust the seasoning and keep warm.

5 Mix together the salad ingredients and place on a large serving plate. Serve the warm chicken breasts on top of the salad, using the marinade as a dressing. Garnish with sesame seeds.

Quick Marinade Ideas

For really tender, tasty chicken, try one of the marinades below. For 4 people, use 450 g (1 lb) skinless chicken breast fillets and slash the flesh. Place in a shallow non-metallic dish and pour the marinade over; cover and refrigerate for at least 4 hours, preferably overnight. Grill, basting with the marinade, for 6-8 minutes each side or until quite tender. Serve with noodles, rice or puréed potatoes.

✦ 30 ml (2 tbsp) each of wholegrain mustard, lemon juice, runny honey and plenty of seasoning.

✦ 45 ml (3 tbsp) lemon juice and 60 ml (4 tbsp) each of orange juice and chopped fresh herbs such as tarragon and parsley, whisked together with 15 ml (1 tbsp) oil, 1 crushed garlic clove and plenty of salt and black pepper.

✦ 30 ml (2 tbsp) soy sauce, 30 ml (2 level tbsp) tomato ketchup, 25 g (1 oz) shredded stem ginger or ginger marmalade, whisked together with 1 crushed garlic clove, 15 ml (1 tbsp) oil, 75 ml (5 tbsp) water and seasoning.

Turkey Escalopes with Asparagus

PREPARATION TIME: 15 MINUTES
COOKING TIME: 20 MINUTES
SERVES 4
370 CALORIES PER SERVING

225 g (8 oz) thin asparagus

2 skinless turkey escalopes, about 225 g (8 oz) each

30 ml (2 level tbsp) plain flour

salt and pepper

15 g (½ oz) butter

15 ml (1 tbsp) oil

300 ml (½ pint) chicken stock

5 ml (1 level tsp) chopped fresh sage or 2.5 ml (½ level tsp) dried sage

60 ml (4 tbsp) dry white wine

150 ml (¼ pint) soured cream

1 Snap off the tough ends of the asparagus spears and trim the spears to equal lengths. Cut off the tips and set aside. Cut each stalk into three pieces.

2 Halve each turkey escalope. Place between two sheets of greaseproof paper, and bat out slightly with a rolling pin. Coat in the flour seasoned with salt and pepper, shaking off any excess.

3 Heat the butter and oil in a large frying pan and fry the turkey until lightly browned on both sides. Add the stock, asparagus stalks, sage and wine, cover and cook gently for 10 minutes. Add the asparagus tips, soured cream and seasoning. Cook for a further 5 minutes. Serve at once.

Turkey Sauté with Lemon and Walnuts

PREPARATION TIME: 10 MINUTES
COOKING TIME: 20 MINUTES
SERVES 4
345 CALORIES PER SERVING

450 g (1 lb) skinless turkey breast fillets

30 ml (2 level tbsp) cornflour

45 ml (3 tbsp) oil

1 green pepper, deseeded and thinly sliced

40 g (1½ oz) walnut halves or pieces

60 ml (4 tbsp) chicken stock

30 ml (2 tbsp) lemon juice

45 ml (3 level tbsp) lemon marmalade

5 ml (1 tsp) white wine vinegar

1.25 ml (¼ tsp) soy sauce

salt and pepper

1 Cut the turkey flesh into 5 cm (2 inch) pencil-thin strips. Put the cornflour in a bowl, add the turkey strips, and toss until coated.

2 Heat half the oil in a large sauté or deep frying pan, add the pepper and walnuts, and fry for 2-3 minutes. Remove from the pan with a slotted spoon.

3 Add the remaining oil to the pan, and fry the turkey strips for 10 minutes or until golden. Add the stock and lemon juice, stirring well. Add the lemon marmalade, vinegar and soy sauce. Season with salt and pepper.

4 Return the walnuts and green pepper to the pan. Cook gently for a further 5 minutes or until the turkey is tender. Taste and adjust the seasoning and serve immediately, garnished with lemon wedges and parsley.

Raspberry Duck

PREPARATION TIME: 10 MINUTES + MARINATING
COOKING TIME: 20 MINUTES
SERVES 2
615 CALORIES PER SERVING

30 ml (2 tbsp) brandy

juice of 2 limes

30 ml (2 tbsp) runny honey

salt and pepper

2 duckling breast fillets, skinned

15 g (½ oz) butter

30 ml (2 tbsp) oil

225 g (8 oz) fresh or frozen raspberries

300 ml (½ pint) rosé wine

1 To make the marinade, mix together the brandy, lime juice, half the honey, and salt and pepper. Place the duck breasts in a shallow dish. Pour the marinade over and leave to stand for 4 hours in a cool place, turning occasionally.

2 Melt the butter with the oil in a frying pan. Remove the breasts from the marinade and fry over high heat for a few minutes. Turn and fry for a further 5 minutes or until cooked.

3 Meanwhile, put the raspberries in a saucepan with the marinade and wine. Heat gently for 5 minutes, then remove one quarter of the raspberries with a slotted spoon and set aside. Add the remaining honey to the pan and boil until reduced to about half.

4 Strain through a sieve, pressing the raspberries with the back of a spoon. Return to the rinsed-out pan with the reserved whole raspberries and reheat. Taste for sweetness and adjust the seasoning. Slice the duck breasts neatly and serve with the sauce.

Duckling Breasts with Armagnac

PREPARATION TIME: 5 MINUTES + MARINATING
COOKING TIME: 25 MINUTES
SERVES 6
240 CALORIES PER SERVING

---

6 duckling breast fillets, 175 g (6 oz) each

---

salt and pepper

---

2 shallots or small onions, skinned and finely chopped

---

2 garlic cloves, skinned and crushed

---

75 ml (5 tbsp) Armagnac

---

fresh thyme sprigs

---

bay leaves

---

fresh herbs, to garnish

---

1 Score the skin on the duckling breasts, and rub with salt. Place side by side in a shallow non-metallic dish.

2 Mix the shallots, garlic and Armagnac, and spoon over the duckling breasts. Add sprigs of fresh thyme, bay leaves and plenty of milled black pepper. Turn the duckling in the marinade, cover and leave to marinate at room temperature for about 1 hour.

3 Place the duckling breasts on a wire rack standing over a roasting tin. Baste with the marinade.

4 Roast in the oven at 230°C (450°F) mark 8 for 10 minutes, then lower the temperature to 200°C (400°F) mark 6 for a further 10-15 minutes.

5 Serve thickly sliced, garnished with fresh herbs.

Crispy Chinese Duck with Oriental Vegetables

PREPARATION TIME: 10 MINUTES
COOKING TIME: 20 MINUTES
SERVES 6
410 CALORIES PER SERVING

125 g (4 oz) each cabbage, carrot, red pepper and cucumber

6 spring onions

6 duck or chicken breasts, about 175 g (6 oz) each

salt and pepper

45 ml (3 tbsp) oil

30 ml (2 tbsp) sesame oil

90 ml (6 level tbsp) yellow bean sauce

45 ml (3 level tbsp) caster sugar

2 garlic cloves, skinned and crushed

1 cm (½ inch) piece of fresh root ginger, peeled and finely chopped

15 ml (1 level tbsp) sesame seeds

75 g (3 oz) baby corn, quartered

1 Cut the cabbage, carrot, red pepper, cucumber and spring onions into fine strips.

2 Prick the skin of the duck breasts well with a fork and rub with salt and pepper. Place on a baking sheet on the top shelf of the oven and cook at 230°C (450°F) mark 8 for 15-20 minutes or until the duck is just cooked, but still pink.

3 Meanwhile, heat 15 ml (1 tbsp) of each oil in a frying pan, add the yellow bean sauce, sugar and 30 ml (2 tbsp) water, and cook for 1 minute. Remove and leave to cool.

4 Heat both remaining oils in the rinsed and dried frying pan. Add the garlic, ginger and sesame seeds, and stir for about 1 minute or until golden brown. Add the cabbage, carrots, pepper and baby corn, and stir-fry briskly for 2-3 minutes. Remove from the heat and stir in the cucumber and spring onions.

5 Carve the duck into slices and arrange on top of the vegetables. Serve immediately with the sauce.

Quick Duck Ideas

Duckling breast fillets are becoming more widely available. They should not be overcooked and are usually served still slightly pink.

✦ Prick duckling skin. Fry over a high heat until browned on both sides. Lower the heat and cook until still a little pink in the centre. Remove and keep warm. Drain most of the fat from the pan. Add a clove of crushed garlic, 15-30 ml (1-2 tbsp) blackcurrant or raspberry jam, a splash of vinegar and a splash of red wine. Bubble for 1-2 minutes, then pour over carved duck and serve.

✦ Cook duck as above and serve with onion and pepper marmalade made by slow-cooking thinly sliced onions in olive oil with a pinch of sugar until soft and caramelised. Add a jar of sliced mixed peppers and plenty of seasoning.

✦ Cook duck as above. Remove from pan and keep warm. Drain off most of the fat. Fry thick apple slices in the residue and arrange on plates with the duck. Deglaze the pan with cider, add a little double cream, bubble for 1-2 minutes, then season and pour over the duck.

Pheasant with Cranberries and Pistachio Nuts

PREPARATION TIME: 10 MINUTES
COOKING TIME: 20 MINUTES
SERVES 6
475 CALORIES PER SERVING

6 pheasant or chicken breast fillets, 175 g (6 oz) each

5 ml (1 level tsp) black pepper

125 g (4 oz) butter

15 ml (1 tbsp) oil

150 g (5 oz) shallots, skinned and roughly chopped

5 ml (1 level tsp) each green and pink peppercorns in brine

200 ml (7 fl oz) Calvados or brandy

450 ml (¾ pint) chicken stock

juice of 1 orange

50 g (2 oz) shelled pistachio nuts

100 g (4 oz) packet of dried cranberries

1 Season the pheasant breasts with pepper. Heat 25 g (1 oz) butter and the oil in a large frying pan. Cook the pheasant breasts, a few at a time, skin side down, for about 5 minutes or until golden brown.

2 Remove the breasts from the pan and place in a single layer in an ovenproof dish. Finish cooking in the oven at 150°C (300°F) mark 2 while you prepare the sauce.

3 Add the shallots and peppercorns to the frying pan and cook, stirring, for 5 minutes. Add 150 ml (5 fl oz) Calvados or brandy, and bubble for 1 minute. Add the chicken stock, orange juice, pistachio nuts and dried cranberries.

Bring to the boil and bubble for 5 minutes. Cut the remaining 75 g (3 oz) butter into small pieces and add a little at a time, whisking after each addition, and keeping the sauce simmering.

4 Return the pheasant breasts to the sauce, pour the remaining Calvados or brandy over and bring back to the boil. Serve immediately.

Flavoured Butters for Chicken

Mash one of the flavour combinations below into softened butter and season with pepper. Shape into a log, wrap in greaseproof paper and keep in the refrigerator. Top hot grilled chicken with a generous slice of butter – wait for it to melt and run over the chicken before serving with vegetables or a crisp green salad.

✦ Chopped chillies and fresh coriander. Remove chilli seeds for a milder flavour.

✦ Grated lime rind and chopped fresh ginger.

✦ Finely chopped rocket or sorrel.

✦ Chopped basil, garlic, sun-dried tomato and capers.

✦ Anchovy, shredded spinach and lemon rind.

✦ Bottled curry paste.

✦ Harissa (from a jar or tube).

✦ Orange rind and juice with chopped chives.

✦ *Fines Herbes* (chopped chervil, tarragon, parsley and chives).

✦ Bottled or homemade green or red pesto.

Quick Chicken Ideas

Ready-prepared skinless, boneless chicken breast fillets are
ideal for a quick supper for 2.

◆ Spread goat's cheese under the skin of chicken breasts and roast with olive oil, a little fresh or dried rosemary and black pepper. Serve with garlic mayonnaise.

◆ Mix thick yogurt, 10 ml (2 tsp) curry paste, crushed garlic and 10 ml (2 tsp) coriander seeds. Slash the chicken breasts and rub with the yogurt mixture. Marinate for 15 minutes, if time, then grill.

◆ Slice chicken breasts into three across the grain. Coat with seasoned flour. Sauté in butter and oil until cooked through. Remove from the pan. Add a clove of crushed garlic and a handful of green beans, sugar snap peas or mangetout to the pan, and cook for 1-2 minutes. Deglaze the pan with a splash of raspberry vinegar and cream. Pour over the chicken and serve.

◆ Soak a small packet of dried porcini or cep mushrooms in 200 ml (7 fl oz) hot water for 15 minutes. Sauté chicken breasts in butter and oil. Add crushed garlic, chopped parsley, soaked mushrooms and their liquid. Cook for 1-2 minutes, then stir in a few spoons of crème fraîche and plenty of chopped parsley.

◆ Cut chicken breasts into strips, then sauté in butter and oil over a high heat until brown. Add half a large can of chopped tomatoes, black olives and 15-30 ml (1-2 tbsp) fresh or bottled pesto. Simmer until the chicken is cooked through.

◆ Fry chopped chicken in butter and oil with chopped onions and garlic, and ground cumin, fenugreek, coriander and cardamom. Add split red lentils and coconut milk. Simmer until chicken is cooked through and lentils are mushy.

Fish and
Shellfish

Kedgeree

PREPARATION TIME: 10 MINUTES
COOKING TIME: 20-25 MINUTES
SERVES 4
425 CALORIES PER SERVING

---

175 g (6 oz) long-grain rice

---

salt

---

450 g (1 lb) smoked haddock fillets

---

2 hard-boiled eggs, shelled

---

50 g (2 oz) butter or margarine

---

cayenne pepper, to taste

---

chopped fresh parsley, to garnish

---

1 Cook the rice in boiling salted water until tender. Drain and rinse in cold running water. Drain well and spread out on a tray to dry.

2 Meanwhile, put the smoked haddock in a large frying pan with just enough water to cover. Bring to simmering point, then simmer for 10-15 minutes or until tender. Drain, skin and flake the fish, discarding any bones.

3 Chop one hard-boiled egg; slice the other and set aside. Melt the butter in a saucepan, add the cooked rice, fish, chopped egg and cayenne pepper to taste. Stir over a moderate heat for about 5 minutes or until hot. Pile on to a warmed serving dish and garnish with parsley and hard-boiled egg slices.

Light Seafood Sauté

PREPARATION TIME: 15 MINUTES
COOKING TIME: 15 MINUTES
SERVES 4
230 CALORIES PER SERVING

30 ml (2 tbsp) oil
450 g (1 lb) monkfish fillet, skinned and cut into bite-sized pieces
1 bunch of spring onions, trimmed and sliced
1 garlic clove, skinned and finely chopped
2.5 cm (1 inch) piece of fresh root ginger, peeled and finely chopped
275 g (10 oz) trimmed leeks, roughly sliced
1 red pepper, deseeded and roughly chopped
125 g (4 oz) cooked peeled prawns
15 ml (1 tbsp) hoisin sauce
15 ml (1 tbsp) light soy sauce
15 ml (1 tbsp) dry sherry
pepper

1 Heat the oil in a large non-stick frying pan, add the monkfish, and sauté for 2-3 minutes. Remove from the pan using a slotted spoon. Add the onions, garlic and ginger to the pan and sauté for 2 minutes or until beginning to soften. Add the leeks and pepper, and sauté for a further 10 minutes or until softened.

2 Return the monkfish to the pan with the prawns, hoisin sauce, soy sauce and sherry. Season with plenty of black pepper (the soy sauce is fairly salty). Cook for 30 seconds-1 minute, stirring. Serve at once.

Seafood Stir-fry

PREPARATION TIME: 15 MINUTES
COOKING TIME: 10 MINUTES
SERVES 4
235 CALORIES PER SERVING

---

45 ml (3 tbsp) groundnut oil

---

350 g (12 oz) Iceberg or Cos lettuce, thinly shredded

---

2 celery sticks, trimmed and cut into thin 5 cm (2 inch) long matchstick strips

---

1 carrot, peeled and sliced into thin 5 cm (2 inch) long matchstick strips

---

350 g (12 oz) haddock or cod fillet, skinned and cut into chunks

---

1 garlic clove, skinned and crushed

---

125 g (4 oz) peeled prawns

---

425 g (15 oz) can of whole baby sweetcorn, drained

---

5 ml (1 tsp) anchovy essence

---

salt and pepper

---

1 Heat 15 ml (1 tbsp) oil in a wok or large frying pan until smoking. Add the lettuce and fry for about 30 seconds or until lightly cooked. Transfer to a serving dish with a slotted spoon and keep warm.

2 Heat the remaining oil in the pan until smoking. Add the celery, carrot, white fish and garlic, and stir-fry over high heat for 2-3 minutes, adding more oil if necessary.

3 Lower the heat and add the prawns, baby sweetcorn and anchovy essence. Toss well together for 2-3 minutes to heat through and coat all the ingredients in the sauce (the fish will flake apart).

4 Add salt and pepper to taste, spoon on top of the lettuce and serve immediately.

Trout Steaks with Coriander

PREPARATION TIME: 15 MINUTES + MARINATING
COOKING TIME: 15 MINUTES
SERVES 4
280 CALORIES PER SERVING

2 rainbow trout, about 350 g (12 oz) each, cleaned

juice of 4 limes

60 ml (4 level tbsp) chopped fresh coriander

1 green chilli, deseeded and sliced (optional)

45 ml (3 tbsp) olive oil

25 g (1 oz) creamed coconut, grated

1 garlic clove, skinned and crushed

salt and pepper

fresh coriander and lime slices, to garnish

1 Thickly slice the trout, discarding heads and tails. In a non-metallic, heat-proof dish, mix the lime juice with the coriander, chilli, oil, coconut and garlic. Add the fish and turn to coat well, then cover and leave to marinate in the refrigerator for about 3 hours.

2 Season well with salt and pepper, and grill, basting occasionally, for 12-15 minutes or until the fish is cooked, turning once. Serve immediately, garnished with coriander and lime slices.

Pink Trout with Almond and Herb Purée

PREPARATION TIME: 20 MINUTES
COOKING TIME: 10-14 MINUTES
SERVES 4
745 CALORIES PER SERVING

4 pink-fleshed trout, about 300 g (10 oz) each, cleaned

50 g (2 oz) butter

15 ml (1 tbsp) lemon juice

10 ml (2 level tsp) paprika

75 g (3 oz) blanched whole almonds

1 garlic clove, skinned

30 ml (2 level tbsp) freshly grated Parmesan cheese

50 g (2 oz) fresh parsley sprigs

150 ml (¼ pint) light olive oil

30 ml (2 tbsp) fromage frais

salt and pepper

parsley sprigs, to garnish

1 Preheat the grill. Rinse the trout and pat dry with absorbent kitchen paper.

2 Put the butter, lemon juice and paprika in a saucepan over a low heat until the butter is melted. With a sharp knife, make diagonal slashes, about 1 cm (½ inch) deep, on both sides of each trout. Lay the trout in a foil-lined grill pan and brush with the paprika butter.

3 Spread the almonds on a baking sheet and place under the grill for 2-3 minutes, turning frequently until toasted and golden. Place 50 g (2 oz) of the toasted almonds in a blender or food processor with the garlic, Parmesan, parsley, olive oil, fromage frais, salt and pepper. Blend until smooth. Roughly chop the remaining almonds and set aside.

4 Grill the trout for 5-7 minutes on each side or until opaque and cooked through, basting from time to time with the paprika butter.

5 Transfer the trout to warmed serving plates. Spoon a good dollop of toasted almond and herb purée on to each plate and scatter over the remaining toasted almonds. Garnish with sprigs of parsley and serve immediately.

NOTE

Pink-fleshed trout has the colour of salmon, but a much more delicate taste.

Flavoured Butters for Grilled Fish

Mash one of the following flavour combinations into softened butter and season with pepper. Shape into a log, wrap in greaseproof paper and keep in the refrigerator. Top hot grilled fish with a generous slice of butter — wait for it to melt and run over the fish before eating.

✦ Anchovy, bottled tapenade and grated onion.

✦ Lemon or lime rind and juice.

✦ Paprika and bottled red pimiento.

✦ Horseradish and fresh parsley.

✦ Fresh chillies and green peppercorns.

Trout with Lime and Saffron Sauce

PREPARATION TIME: 20 MINUTES
COOKING TIME: 15 MINUTES
SERVES 6
405 CALORIES PER SERVING

---

2 limes

---

3 oranges

---

75 ml (3 fl oz) sunflower oil

---

25 ml (1 fl oz) white wine vinegar

---

pinch of saffron strands

---

salt and pepper

---

9 skinless trout fillets, about 75 g (3 oz) each

---

10 ml (2 level tsp) red lumpfish or salmon roe

---

30 ml (2 level tbsp) mixed chopped fresh parsley, tarragon, chives and dill

---

dill sprigs, to garnish

---

1 Cut away the peel and pith from 1 lime and all the oranges. Slice the flesh. Squeeze the juice from the remaining lime and put 25 ml (1 fl oz) in a large shallow pan with the oil, vinegar, saffron and seasoning.

2 Cut the trout fillets in half lengthways to give 18 pieces. Twist three fillets together into a knot and secure with a wooden cocktail stick.

3 Place the trout on a wire rack over a frying pan or roasting tin of simmering water. Cover with a tent of foil and cook for 6-7 minutes or until just cooked.

4 Meanwhile, bring the sauce to the boil, then remove from the heat and add the lime and orange slices, the lumpfish roe and chopped herbs. Serve the trout with the warm sauce spooned over. Garnish with dill sprigs.

Roast Salmon in Mustard Butter

PREPARATION TIME: 10 MINUTES
COOKING TIME: 20 MINUTES
SERVES 6
560 CALORIES PER SERVING

1.1 kg (2½ lb) piece of boned middle cut of salmon

175 g (6 oz) butter, melted

45 ml (3 level tbsp) wholegrain mustard

20 ml (4 level tsp) dried dill weed

salt and pepper

300 g (10 oz) fresh spinach, rocket or mixed salad leaves

1 Open out the salmon like a book until almost flat, pressing along the backbone area. Place the salmon, skin side up, in a shallow ovenproof dish just large enough to hold it.

2 Mix together the butter, mustard, dill and seasoning. Pour over the salmon. Cook in the oven at 230°C (450°F) mark 8 for about 20 minutes or until just tender.

3 Toss the salad leaves together and season well. Place on large plates.

4 Cut the salmon into thick slices and serve on top of the leaves with the mustard butter spooned over.

Salmon en Papillote

PREPARATION TIME: 5-10 MINUTES
COOKING TIME: 20-25 MINUTES
SERVES 4
340 CALORIES PER SERVING

25 g (1 oz) butter

125 g (4 oz) mangetout, trimmed and sliced diagonally

4 salmon fillets or steaks, about 150 g (5 oz) each

1 large orange

30 ml (2 level tbsp) chopped fresh parlsey

15 ml (1 level tbsp) capers, drained and rinsed

salt and pepper

1 Cut four rounds of greaseproof paper 30 cm (12 inches) in diameter. Smear the centres with half the butter, divide the mangetout among them and top with the salmon fillets.

2 Pare one or two thin strips of rind from the orange and cut into thin slivers. Grate the remaining rind over the fish. Scatter the strips of rind over the fish with the parsley and capers. Add salt and pepper to taste.

3 Squeeze the juice from the orange over the fillets, dot with the remaining butter, then fold over the edges of the paper to enclose the fish completely. Roll over the edges to seal. Transfer the parcels to a baking sheet and bake in the oven at 190°C (375°F) mark 5 for 20-25 minutes. Serve hot.

Spiced BBQ Salmon

PREPARATION TIME: 15 MINUTES
COOKING TIME: 15 MINUTES
SERVES 6
295 CALORIES PER SERVING

---

900 g (2 lb) salmon fillet, with skin on and scales removed

---

6 cardamom pods

---

5 ml (1 level tsp) cumin seeds

---

5 ml (1 level tsp) coriander seeds

2.5 ml (½ level tsp) black peppercorns

2.5 ml (½ level tsp) coarse salt

---

30 ml (2 tbsp) olive oil

---

1 Remove any remaining salmon bones with tweezers. Using a sharp knife, slash the skin side into diamonds.

2 Remove the dark seeds from the cardamom pods and discard the pods. Finely grind the seeds with the cumin seeds, coriander seeds, peppercorns and coarse salt in a grinder or in a strong bowl with the end of a rolling pin.

3 Brush the salmon with oil and press the spices firmly on to the skin side. If cooking on a barbecue, place the salmon in a fish griller and cook for 10-15 minutes, turning halfway through. To cook in the oven, place the salmon on an oiled baking sheet and cook at 230°C (450°F) mark 8 for 10-15 minutes or until brown and crisp but just cooked on the inside.

Roast Salmon with a Peanut Crust

PREPARATION TIME: 5 MINUTES
COOKING TIME: 20 MINUTES
SERVES 4
865 CALORIES PER SERVING

---

1 red chilli, deseeded and finely chopped

2.5 cm (1 inch) piece of fresh root ginger, peeled and grated

---

175 g (6 oz) unsalted butter, softened

---

45 ml (3 level tbsp) chopped fresh parsley

---

finely grated rind of 1 lime

---

75 g (3 oz) salted roasted peanuts

---

125 g (4 oz) fresh white breadcrumbs

3-4 spring onions, trimmed and finely chopped

---

salt and pepper

---

4 salmon fillets, about 175 g (6 oz) each (skinned if wished)

---

1 Beat the chilli and ginger into the unsalted butter with the parsley and lime rind. Roughly process the peanuts in a blender.

2 Fry the breadcrumbs with the spring onions and peanuts in 50 g (2 oz) of the flavoured butter until golden, stirring continuously to prevent the bread-crumbs sticking together. Season with salt and pepper.

3 Arrange the salmon fillets, skin side uppermost, in a roasting tin. Spoon the fried breadcrumb mixture on the top. Cook in the oven at 200°C (400°F) mark 6 for 10-15 minutes or until the salmon is just cooked. Melt the remaining flavoured butter and serve with the roast salmon.

COOK'S TIP

To save time, make up a batch of the flavoured butter and the fried peanut and breadcrumb topping, and freeze ahead. Both of these mixtures can be used direct from the freezer; just allow an extra 2-3 minutes' cooking time at step 3.

Cod with Crunchy Herb Topping

PREPARATION TIME: 5 MINUTES
COOKING TIME: 10-15 MINUTES
SERVES 4
380 CALORIES PER SERVING

45 ml (3 tbsp) olive oil

75 g (3 oz) fresh white breadcrumbs

1 garlic clove, skinned and crushed

60 ml (4 level tbsp) chopped fresh parsley

60 ml (4 level tbsp) chopped sun-dried tomatoes in oil, drained

30 ml (2 level tbsp) freshly grated Parmesan cheese

salt and pepper

4 skinless cod fillets, each weighing about 150 g (5 oz)

flat-leaf parsley sprigs, to garnish

1 Heat 30 ml (2 tbsp) oil in a frying pan, add the breadcrumbs and garlic, and fry for 2-3 minutes or until the breadcrumbs are golden and crisp. Add the parsley, tomatoes and cheese, season with salt and pepper and mix well.

2 Arrange the cod fillets in a flameproof baking dish, brush with a little oil and cook under a fairly hot grill for 5 minutes.

3 Turn the fish over and grill for 3-5 minutes or until just cooked. Spoon the topping over and grill for a further 1-2 minutes or until crisp and golden. Serve at once, garnished with flat-leaf parsley sprigs.

Grilled Sardines with Fresh Tomato Sauce

PREPARATION TIME: 10 MINUTES
COOKING TIME: 20-25 MINUTES
SERVES 4
270 CALORIES PER SERVING

16 small or 8 large sardines, cleaned

30 ml (2 tbsp) olive oil

a few fresh thyme sprigs

juice of ½ lemon

lemon rind shreds, to garnish

For the tomato sauce

15 ml (1 tbsp) olive oil

1 small onion, skinned and finely chopped

1 garlic clove, skinned and finely chopped

450 g (1 lb) ripe tomatoes, finely chopped

15 ml (1 level tbsp) chopped fresh parsley

salt and pepper

1 To make the tomato sauce, heat the oil in a saucepan, add the onion and garlic and fry gently until the onion is softened. Add the tomatoes and parsley, then season. Cook, uncovered, for 10-15 minutes.

2 Meanwhile, score the fish with three or four diagonal cuts on each side. Brush with oil, and push a few sprigs of thyme into some of the cuts. Season with pepper and sprinkle with lemon juice.

3 Arrange the fish on the grill rack and grill for about 4 minutes on each side or until cooked, brushing frequently with the oil and juices.

4 Arrange the cooked sardines on a platter, and pour over any juices from the grill pan. Garnish with lemon rind shreds, and serve with the tomato sauce.

Grilled Plaice with Mushrooms

PREPARATION TIME: 20 MINUTES
COOKING TIME: 10 MINUTES
SERVES 4
215 CALORIES PER SERVING

25 g (1 oz) butter or margarine

225 g (8 oz) button mushrooms, wiped and finely chopped

125 g (4 oz) eating apple, peeled, cored and chopped

25 g (1 oz) fresh brown breadcrumbs

5 ml (1 level tsp) wholegrain mustard

30 ml (2 level tbsp) chopped fresh parsley

salt and pepper

4 plaice fillets, about 125 g (4 oz) each, skinned

60 ml (4 tbsp) dry cider

apple slices, to garnish

1 Melt the butter in a small saucepan and sauté the mushrooms and apple for 2-3 minutes. Increase the heat and cook, stirring, for 1-2 minutes, until most of the excess liquid has evaporated.

2 Off the heat, stir in the breadcrumbs, half the wholegrain mustard and the chopped parsley. Season with salt and pepper.

3 Divide the mixture between the plaice fillets and roll up, skinned side inside. Secure with wooden cocktail sticks. Place the rolled plaice fillets, seam side down, in a small shallow flameproof dish.

4 Whisk together the remaining mustard and the cider. Spoon over the fish. Grill for about 10 minutes, turning occasionally and brushing with the mustard mixture.

5 Remove the cocktail sticks. Serve garnished with apple slices.

Grilled Turbot with Chervil and Tomato Sauce

PREPARATION TIME: 20 MINUTES
COOKING TIME: 10-12 MINUTES
SERVES 4
280 CALORIES PER SERVING

---

300 ml (½ pint) milk

---

1 onion slice

---

1 mace blade

4-6 black peppercorns

---

2 tomatoes

---

25 g (1 oz) butter

---

scant 15 g (½ oz) plain flour

---

salt and pepper

---

5 ml (1 level tsp) tomato purée

---

60 ml (4 level tbsp) chopped fresh chervil

---

4 turbot steaks, about 175 g (6 oz) each

---

lemon juice, to taste

---

chervil sprigs, to garnish

---

1 Put the milk in a small saucepan with the onion, mace and peppercorns. Bring to the boil and remove from the heat. Leave to infuse for 10 minutes, then strain.

2 Immerse the tomatoes in boiling water for 15-30 seconds, then remove and peel away the skins. Cut the flesh into strips, discarding the seeds.

3 Melt 15 g (½ oz) butter in a small saucepan. Stir in the flour and cook for 1 minute. Off the heat, gradually stir in the strained milk. Season with salt and pepper.

4 Bring the sauce to the boil, stirring constantly. Simmer gently for a few minutes. Whisk in the tomato purée and chopped chervil.

5 Meanwhile, melt the remaining butter. Halve the turbot steaks, brush with melted butter and grill for 5-6 minutes on each side.

6 Add the tomato strips to the sauce. Reheat gently, stirring in lemon juice to taste. Garnish the turbot with chervil and serve with the sauce.

Fish Cakes with Herbs

PREPARATION TIME: 15 MINUTES
COOKING TIME: 10 MINUTES
SERVES 4
175 CALORIES PER SERVING

275 g (10 oz) haddock fillet, skinned
15 ml (1 tbsp) lemon juice
15 ml (1 tbsp) Worcestershire sauce
15 ml (1 level tbsp) creamed horseradish
100 ml (4 fl oz) milk
15 ml (1 level tbsp) snipped chives
15 ml (1 level tbsp) chopped fresh parsley
350 g (12 oz) cooked potatoes, mashed
50 g (2 oz) fresh wholemeal breadcrumbs

1 Put the fish in a blender or food processor with the lemon juice, Worcestershire sauce and horseradish, and blend until smooth. Transfer to a bowl and stir in the milk, herbs and potatoes until evenly blended.

2 Shape the mixture into four fish cakes. Coat with breadcrumbs.

3 Grill the fish cakes under a moderate heat for 5 minutes on each side, until browned.

Stuffed Rolled Sole

PREPARATION TIME: 5 MINUTES
COOKING TIME: 25 MINUTES
SERVES 6
380 CALORIES PER SERVING

---

75 g (3 oz) butter

½ onion, skinned and chopped

---

225 g (8 oz) button mushrooms, wiped and trimmed

---

75 g (3 oz) fresh white breadcrumbs

---

finely grated rind of 1 lemon

---

15 ml (1 level tbsp) chopped fresh tarragon leaves

---

salt and pepper

---

18 lemon sole quarter-cut fillets (two from each side of the
fish), skinned

---

300 ml (½ pint) dry white wine

---

150 ml (¼ pint) water

---

30 ml (2 level tbsp) plain flour

---

90 ml (6 level tbsp) double cream, at room temperature

---

fresh tarragon sprigs, to garnish

---

1 To make the stuffing, melt 25 g (1 oz) of the butter in a saucepan. Add the onion and fry gently until lightly coloured.

2 Meanwhile, finely slice half the mushrooms and reserve. Chop the remainder very finely. Put the chopped mushrooms in a bowl with the breadcrumbs, lemon rind and tarragon.

3 Add the softened onion and season with salt and pepper. Stir well until combined.

4 Place a sole fillet, skinned-side uppermost, on a board. Put a teaspoonful of stuffing on one end of the fillet. Roll the fish up around it and secure with a cocktail stick.

5 Stand the fish upright in a well-buttered baking dish. Repeat with the remaining sole fillets, placing them side by side in the dish. Mix together the wine and water, and pour over the fish. Cover loosely and bake in the oven at 190°C (375°F) mark 5 for 15 minutes.

6 Remove the fish from the cooking liquid with a slotted spoon and discard the cocktail sticks. Place the fish in a single layer in a warmed serving dish, cover and keep warm. Strain the liquid into a jug.

7 Melt 25 g (1 oz) butter in a saucepan, sprinkle in the flour and cook for 1-2 minutes, stirring. Remove from the heat, then gradually stir in the strained cooking liquid. Bring to the boil, reduce the heat and simmer gently for 5 minutes, stirring until thick.

8 Meanwhile, melt the remaining butter in a frying pan, add the finely sliced mushrooms and fry gently. Whisk the cream into the sauce. Pour a little sauce over each rolled fillet, then garnish with the sliced mushrooms and tarragon sprigs. Pour any remaining sauce into a warmed sauceboat and serve separately.

Sweet and Sour Fish

PREPARATION TIME: 10 MINUTES
COOKING TIME: 10-12 MINUTES
SERVES 4
175 CALORIES PER SERVING

4 cod fillets, about 150 g (5 oz) each, skinned

15 ml (1 tbsp) soy sauce

30 ml (2 tbsp) lemon juice

10 ml (2 tsp) white wine vinegar

15 ml (1 tbsp) runny honey

10 ml (2 tsp) tomato ketchup

1 garlic clove, skinned and crushed

1.25 ml (¼ level tsp) paprika

oil

1 red pepper, deseeded and sliced

125 g (4 oz) spring onions, trimmed and sliced

125 g (4 oz) button mushrooms, wiped (optional)

125 g (4 oz) frozen green beans or mangetout

pepper

1 Divide each piece of fish in half. Roll up neatly with the skinned sides inside.

2 Mix together the soy sauce, lemon juice, vinegar, honey, ketchup, garlic and paprika and place in a large frying pan. Add the fish and baste with the sauce. Bring to a very gentle simmer, then cover and cook for 10-12 minutes or until tender.

3 Meanwhile, heat a little oil in another frying pan. Stir-fry the vegetables over a high heat for 3-4 minutes or until just tender. Season with pepper and transfer to a serving dish.

4 Transfer the fish to the serving dish, spoon the sauce over and serve.

Cod and Crab Gratin

PREPARATION TIME: 15 MINUTES
COOKING TIME: 15 MINUTES
SERVES 4
445 CALORIES PER SERVING

about 700 g (1½ lb) medium new potatoes, scrubbed

450 g (1 lb) cod fillet

300 ml (½ pint) milk

salt and pepper

225 g (8 oz) small button mushrooms, wiped

25 g (1 oz) butter or margarine

25 g (1 oz) plain flour

25 g (1 oz) each white and dark crab meat

10 ml (2 level tsp) Dijon mustard

75 g (3 oz) Cheddar cheese, grated

1 Boil the potatoes in their skins until tender. Drain, then slice thickly.

2 Meanwhile, skin the cod fillet and cut the flesh into 2.5 cm (1 inch) pieces.

3 Place the fish in a saucepan with the milk and seasoning. Bring to the boil, then reduce the heat, cover and simmer for 5 minutes. Add the mushrooms, re-cover and simmer for a further 5 minutes, or until the fish is tender. Strain off and reserve the milk. Place the fish and mushrooms in a shallow flame-proof dish, cover and keep warm.

4 Melt the butter in a small saucepan. Stir in the flour and cook for 1 minute. Off the heat, gradually stir in the reserved milk. Cook, stirring, for 2-3 minutes or until thickened and smooth. Stir in the crab meat, mustard and seasoning and heat through gently.

5 Pour the sauce over the cod and mushrooms, stirring gently to mix. Level the surface with a knife. Top with slices of potato and scatter over the grated cheese. Grill until golden and bubbling. Serve immediately.

Mixed Seafood Gratin

PREPARATION TIME: **10** MINUTES
COOKING TIME: **20** MINUTES
SERVES **4**
800 CALORIES PER SERVING

---

450 g (1 lb) mixed seafood, such as cod, cooked mussels and
cooked prawns

---

50 g (2 oz) butter

---

50 g (2 oz) onion, skinned and roughly chopped

---

2 garlic cloves, skinned and crushed

---

15 ml (1 level tbsp) plain flour

---

100 ml (4 fl oz) white wine

---

50 ml (2 fl oz) milk

---

142 ml (5 fl oz) carton of double cream

---

175 g (6 oz) Emmental cheese, grated

---

125 g (4 oz) watercress, finely chopped

---

salt and pepper

---

50 g (2 oz) fresh breadcrumbs

---

125 g (4 oz) plain tortilla chips, crumbled

---

shredded leeks, to serve (see Cook's Tip)

---

1 Cut the cod, if using, into bite-sized pieces.

2 Melt the butter in a large saucepan, add the onion and garlic, and sauté for 2-3 minutes. Add the flour and cook, stirring, for 1 minute. Pour in the wine and milk, and bring to the boil, stirring all the time. Add the cod and simmer for 5-6 minutes. Add the cream and remove from the heat.

3 Add 125 g (4 oz) grated cheese, the mussels, prawns and watercress to the sauce. Season with salt and pepper. Place over a gentle heat and bring to simmering point, then immediately spoon into a shallow, overproof dish.

4 Mix the breadcrumbs, remaining cheese and crumbled tortilla chips together. Sprinkle over the fish, then grill until golden and bubbling. Serve with shredded leeks.

COOK'S TIP

For the quickest, tastiest accompaniment, shred about 450 g (1 lb) leeks very finely and cook in boiling salted water for 1 minute only. Drain well and season with salt and pepper. Serve immediately.

Oysters au Gratin

PREPARATION TIME: 20 MINUTES
COOKING TIME: 10 MINUTES
SERVES 4-6
220-150 CALORIES PER SERVING

50 g (2 oz) streaky bacon, derinded and finely chopped

75 g (3 oz) celery, trimmed and finely chopped

200 g (7 oz) can of artichoke hearts, drained and finely chopped

12 large oysters

200 g (7 oz) Mozzarella cheese, thinly sliced

1 In a small frying pan, fry the bacon until the fat begins to run. Add the celery and artichokes, and cook, stirring, for 2 minutes. Leave to cool.

2 Scrub the oyster shells well. Open the oysters by inserting an oyster knife into the hinge linking the shells and cutting through the muscle. Prise the shells apart; discard the flatter shell from each oyster.

3 Spoon a little of the bacon and artichoke mixture over each oyster.

4 Top with cheese. Cook under a medium grill for 10 minutes.

Seafood Parisienne

PREPARATION TIME: 5 MINUTES
COOKING TIME: 5-10 MINUTES
SERVES 4
215 CALORIES PER SERVING

227 g (8 oz) pack of ready-cooked seafood cocktail (see Note)

75 ml (3 fl oz) white wine

150 ml (¼ pint) water

2-3 parsley stalks

1 bay leaf

6 peppercorns

40 g (1½ oz) butter

1 shallot, skinned and finely chopped

125 g (4 oz) button mushrooms, wiped and halved

30 ml (2 level tbsp) plain flour

75 ml (3 fl oz) milk

30 ml (2 tbsp) single cream

salt and pepper

30 ml (2 level tbsp) fresh breadcrumbs

bay leaves, to garnish

1 Put the seafood in a saucepan with the wine, water, parsley stalks, bay leaf and peppercorns. Simmer very gently for 2-3 minutes, then lift out the seafood with a slotted spoon and set aside. Discard the bay leaf and peppercorns. Remove the parsley stalks and reserve. Reserve the cooking liquid.

2 Melt 25 g (1 oz) butter in a saucepan, add the shallot and mushrooms, and cook for 3-5 minutes or until softened. Add the flour and cook gently for 1 minute, stirring. Gradually stir in the cooking liquid, bring to the boil and cook, stirring constantly, until thickened. Stir in the milk and boil until reduced slightly.

3 Chop the reserved parsley stalks and stir into the sauce with the cream and seafood. Season to taste and spoon into small gratin dishes or scrubbed, deep scallop shells, if wished. Scatter over the breadcrumbs, dot with the remaining butter and grill until browned and bubbling. Serve at once, garnished with bay leaves.

NOTE

Packs of ready-cooked chilled or frozen seafood cocktail are available from major supermarkets. They usually include cooked mussels, squid, prawns and sometimes cockles.

Prawns Fried in Garlic

PREPARATION TIME: 5 MINUTES
COOKING TIME: 5 MINUTES
SERVES 2
460 CALORIES PER SERVING

50 g (2 oz) butter
30 ml (2 tbsp) olive oil
12 raw Dublin Bay prawns in shells
3 garlic cloves, skinned and crushed
60 ml (4 tbsp) brandy
salt and pepper
lemon wedges, to garnish

1 Melt the butter with the oil in a large heavy-based pan. Add the prawns and garlic, and fry over a high heat for 5 minutes, tossing the prawns constantly.

2 Sprinkle the brandy over the prawns and season with salt and pepper. Serve immediately, garnished with lemon wedges.

Scallops with Ginger

PREPARATION TIME: 15 MINUTES
COOKING TIME: 3 MINUTES
SERVES 3
280 CALORIES PER SERVING

450 g (1 lb) shelled large scallops

30 ml (2 tbsp) oil

4 celery sticks, sliced diagonally

1 bunch of spring onions, trimmed and sliced diagonally

25 g (1 oz) piece of fresh root ginger, peeled and sliced

2 large garlic cloves, skinned and sliced

1.25 ml (¼ level tsp) chilli powder

30 ml (2 tbsp) lemon juice

30 ml (2 tbsp) soy sauce

45 ml (3 level tbsp) chopped fresh coriander

salt and pepper

1 Cut the scallops into 5 mm (¼ inch) slices.

2 Heat the oil in a large wok or frying pan. Add the scallops, celery, onions, ginger, garlic and chilli powder, and stir-fry over a high heat for 2 minutes or until just tender.

3 Pour in the lemon juice and soy sauce, allow to bubble up, then stir in about 30 ml (2 level tbsp) chopped coriander and seasoning. Serve immediately, topped with the remaining coriander.

Prawns with Spinach

PREPARATION TIME: 5 MINUTES
COOKING TIME: 22 MINUTES
SERVES 4
340 CALORIES PER SERVING

60 ml (4 tbsp) ghee or vegetable oil

1 small onion, skinned and finely chopped

10 ml (2 level tsp) ground ginger

10 ml (2 level tsp) garam masala

5 ml (1 level tsp) mustard seeds

2.5 ml (½ level tsp) chilli powder

2.5 ml (½ level tsp) ground turmeric

400 g (14 oz) frozen cooked peeled prawns, thawed and
thoroughly dried

450 g (1 lb) frozen leaf spinach

60 ml (4 level tbsp) desiccated coconut

5 ml (1 level tsp) salt

1 Heat half the ghee or oil in a heavy-based saucepan or flameproof casserole, add the onion, and fry gently for about 5 minutes or until soft.

2 Add the spices and fry, stirring, for a further 2 minutes. Add the prawns, increase the heat and toss to coat in the spiced onion mixture. Remove with a slotted spoon and set aside.

3 Heat the remaining ghee or oil in the pan, add the spinach and heat gently until thawed. Stir frequently and cook for 8-10 minutes, or according to packet instructions.

4 Return the prawns to the pan, add half the coconut and the salt and fold gently to mix. Cook for 5 minutes to allow the flavours to mingle, then transfer to a warmed serving dish. Sprinkle with the remaining coconut and serve immediately.

Mussels in White Wine

PREPARATION TIME: 15 MINUTES
COOKING TIME: 5 MINUTES
SERVES 4-6
225-150 CALORIES PER SERVING

---

1 shallot, skinned and finely chopped

---

25 g (1 oz) celery, trimmed and finely chopped

---

100 ml (4 fl oz) dry white wine

1.4 kg (3 lb) mussels, cleaned

---

15 ml (1 level tbsp) chopped fresh parsley

---

100 ml (4 fl oz) double cream

---

pepper

---

warm crusty bread, to serve

---

1 Put the shallot and celery in a saucepan with the wine and bring to the boil. Add the mussels and cover the pan with a close-fitting lid. Cook over a high heat for about 5 minutes, shaking the pan frequently, until the mussel shells are open.

2 Remove from the heat and discard any mussels that have not opened. Discard the one loose shell from each mussel. Put the mussels on their half-shell into a warmed dish or individual cocottes. Keep warm.

3 Strain the cooking liquid through a sieve lined with absorbent kitchen paper. Return to the pan and add the parsley, cream and pepper to taste. Bring just to boiling point, then pour over the mussels.

4 Serve immediately, accompanied by warm crusty bread.

Seafood Paella

PREPARATION TIME: 10 MINUTES
COOKING TIME: 25 MINUTES
SERVES 6
295 CALORIES PER SERVING

---

30 ml (2 tbsp) olive oil

---

8 spring onions, trimmed and chopped (optional)

---

3 garlic cloves, skinned and crushed

---

225 g (8 oz) long-grain white rice

---

pinch of saffron strands or 2.5 ml (½ level tsp) ground turmeric

---

2 fish stock cubes or 600 ml (1 pint) fish stock

---

400 g (14 oz) can of chopped tomatoes, drained

---

450 g (1 lb) ready-cooked seafood cocktail (see page 133)

---

225 g (8 oz) frozen peas

---

1 small red pepper, deseeded and sliced

---

salt and pepper

---

fresh parsley or coriander, to garnish

---

1 Heat the olive oil in a large saucepan. Add the spring onions, if using, and the garlic and cook for 2 minutes. Stir in the rice and saffron or turmeric and cook for 1 minute.

2 Crumble the stock cubes into a jug and make up to 600 ml (1 pint) with boiling water. Stir well until the stock cubes are completely dissolved, then add to the pan with the drained tomatoes. Alternatively, use 600 ml (1 pint) prepared fish stock. Bring to the boil, then simmer, uncovered, for 12 minutes, stirring occasionally.

3 Stir in the seafood, peas and red pepper until evenly mixed. Season well with salt and pepper. Simmer for a further 10 minutes, stirring frequently, until all the liquid has been absorbed and the rice is tender. Serve garnished with parsley or coriander sprigs.

Quick Grilled Fish Ideas

Spice up grilled fish with one of the following:

✦ While the fish is grilling, make a quick caponata by sautéing onions, peppers, courgettes and celery in a little oil until softened. Moisten with chopped canned tomatoes and flavour with garlic, capers and fresh herbs. Serve the grilled fish on a bed of caponata.

✦ Flavour 150 ml (¼ pint) mayonnaise with 15-30 ml (1-2 tbsp) creamed horseradish and fresh parsley, or garlic, mustard, gherkins, black olives and pickled chillies, or your favourite fresh herbs or watercress. Serve a dollop with the fish.

✦ Sauté 1-2 cloves chopped garlic, 125 g (4 oz) sliced mushrooms and a large pinch of dried thyme with a dried chilli (if you like). Drain and rinse a can of lentils, and add to the mushrooms with a little stock or water to moisten. Heat through. Spoon on to plates and top with the grilled fish.

✦ Finely chop 2 ripe tomatoes and heat through with 75 ml (5 tbsp) bottled French dressing, a squeeze of lemon juice, plenty of shredded basil and salt and pepper. Pour over the grilled fish.

✦ Blanch green beans, sugar snap peas, mangetout or asparagus. Toss with 45 ml (3 tbsp) French dressing flavoured with 15 ml (1 tbsp) pesto and a few black olives or artichoke hearts. Arrange the grilled fish on top and drizzle a little extra dressing with pesto on top, along with plenty of black pepper.

✦ Make a spicy salsa with a finely chopped onion, 1-2 green chillies, a handful of fresh coriander, a little chopped cucumber and 2 fresh tomatoes. Toss with a spoonful of lime juice and a spoonful of oil and plenty of seasoning. Serve this and a dollop of guacamole with the fish.

✦ Cook thoroughly washed fresh spinach in the water clinging to its leaves. Drain and toss with butter, crushed garlic, pine nuts and raisins. Season with nutmeg and paprika. Divide between serving plates and top with the fish and a little more nutmeg and paprika.

Pasta and Noodles

Spaghetti alla Carbonara

PREPARATION TIME: ABOUT 15 MINUTES
COOKING TIME: ABOUT 7 MINUTES
SERVES 4-6
675-450 CALORIES PER SERVING

125-150 g (4-5 oz) smoked pancetta, in slices

1 garlic clove, skinned

30 ml (2 tbsp) extra-virgin olive oil

25 g (1 oz) butter

3 eggs

30 ml (2 level tbsp) chopped fresh parsley

30 ml (2 tbsp) dry white wine

40 g (1½ oz) Parmesan cheese, grated

40 g (1½ oz) pecorino cheese, grated

salt and pepper

400 g (14 oz) spaghetti

1 Remove the rind from the pancetta, then cut into tiny strips. Halve the garlic. Heat the oil and butter in a heavy-based pan. Add the pancetta and garlic and cook over a medium heat for 3-4 minutes or until the pancetta begins to crisp. Turn off the heat; discard the garlic.

2 Meanwhile, in a mixing bowl large enough to hold the cooked spaghetti later, beat the eggs with the parsley, wine and half of each of the cheeses. Season with salt and pepper.

3 Cook the spaghetti in a large pan of boiling salted water until *al dente* (tender but still firm to the bite), or according to packet instructions.

4 When the spaghetti is almost cooked, gently reheat the pancetta in the pan. Drain the spaghetti thoroughly, then immediately add to the egg mixture in the bowl with the pancetta. Toss well to cook the eggs until they are creamy. Add the remaining cheeses, toss lightly and serve at once.

Spaghetti with smoked salmon and scrambled eggs is prepared in a similar way. Omit the pancetta and garlic. Instead, add 125 g (4 oz) smoked salmon strips to the egg mixture at step 2. Heat the butter and oil and add with the pasta at step 4. Finish as above, adding the cheese and tossing in the same way.

Fusilli with Mushrooms

PREPARATION TIME: 10 MINUTES
COOKING TIME: 15 MINUTES
SERVES 4
500 CALORIES PER SERVING

30 ml (2 tbsp) olive oil
225 g (8 oz) brown cap mushrooms, wiped and roughly chopped
2 garlic cloves, skinned and crushed
45 ml (3 level tbsp) black olive paste
10 ml (2 level tsp) chilli paste
60 ml (4 level tbsp) chopped fresh parsley
60 ml (4 tbsp) mascarpone cheese
salt and pepper
400 g (14 oz) dried fusilli

1 Heat the oil in a frying pan, add the mushrooms and garlic, and cook for 3-4 minutes or until most of the liquid has evaporated. Remove from the heat and stir in the olive paste, chilli paste, parsley and mascarpone. Season with salt and pepper, bearing in mind that the olive paste is quite salty.

2 Cook the pasta in a large pan of boiling salted water for 10-12 minutes or until al dente (tender but still slightly firm). Drain well and return to the pan. Reheat the sauce briefly, if necessary, and stir in the pasta. Serve at once.

Pork and Pasta Sauté

PREPARATION TIME: 15 MINUTES + MARINATING
COOKING TIME: 15-20 MINUTES
SERVES 4
445 CALORIES PER SERVING

---

450 g (1 lb) pork fillet

---

4 rashers of streaky bacon, derinded and chopped

---

2 red onions, skinned and finely sliced

---

15 ml (1 level tbsp) wholegrain mustard

---

100 ml (4 fl oz) dry cider

---

1 garlic clove, skinned and crushed

45-60 ml (3-4 tbsp) oil

---

salt and pepper

---

1 green pepper, deseeded and cut into strips

---

175 g (6 oz) green beans, halved

---

75 g (3 oz) dried pasta shells or bows

---

15 ml (1 tbsp) soy sauce

---

60 ml (4 tbsp) light stock

---

1 Trim the pork and cut into strips, about 5 cm x 5 mm (2 x ¼ inch), discarding any excess fat.

2 Put the pork, bacon and onions in a bowl. Add the mustard, cider, garlic and 15 ml (1 tbsp) oil. Season with salt and pepper and stir well. Cover and leave to marinate in the refrigerator for at least 1 hour, preferably overnight.

3 Blanch the green pepper and beans together in boiling salted water for 2 minutes, then drain. Rinse under cold running water and leave to cool.

4 Cook the pasta in boiling salted water for 7-10 minutes or until just cooked. Drain and toss in a little oil to prevent the pasta sticking.

5 Remove the pork, bacon and onions from the marinade, reserving the marinade. Heat 30 ml (2 tbsp) oil in a large frying pan. Add the meat and onions and sauté over a high heat for 3-4 minutes or until lightly browned.

6 Stir in the beans and green pepper with the marinade, soy sauce and stock. Season to taste with pepper. Bring to the boil, stirring, then simmer gently for about 4 minutes. Add the pasta and cook for 1 minute or until piping hot. Serve immediately.

Three Cheese Pasta

PREPARATION TIME: 5 MINUTES
COOKING TIME: 5 MINUTES
SERVES 4
770 CALORIES PER SERVING

350 g (12 oz) fresh white spaghetti
salt
40 g (1½ oz) unsalted butter
75 g (3 oz) dolcelatte, cut into small cubes
175 g (6 oz) mascarpone cheese
75 g (3 oz) Parmesan cheese, grated
40 g (1½ oz) walnuts, chopped
15 ml (1 level tbsp) snipped fresh chives

1 Cook the pasta in boiling salted water for 3-5 minutes or until *al dente* (tender but still firm to the bite). Meanwhile, melt the butter in a pan, add the dolcelatte and mascarpone cheeses and heat gently until melted.

2 Drain the pasta thoroughly and stir in the melted cheese mixture. Scatter the Parmesan, walnuts and chives over the top, toss and serve.

Spaghetti with Clams

PREPARATION TIME: 15 MINUTES
COOKING TIME: ABOUT 8 MINUTES
SERVES 4-6
685-460 CALORIES PER SERVING

---

700 g (1½ lb) venus or baby clams in shells

---

3 garlic cloves, skinned

2.5 ml (½ level tsp) dried chilli flakes

---

350 g (12 oz) plum tomatoes (or other flavourful tomatoes)

---

75 ml (5 tbsp) extra-virgin olive oil

---

100 ml (4 fl oz) dry white wine

---

salt and pepper

---

400 g (14 oz) dried spaghetti

---

30 ml (2 level tbsp) chopped fresh parsley

---

40 g (1½ oz) butter

---

1 Wash the clams in plenty of cold water and scrub the shells with a small brush. Leave to soak in a bowl of fresh cold water for 10 minutes, then rinse again and drain well. Discard any clams which do not close if their shells are tapped firmly.

2 Finely chop the garlic cloves and crush the chilli flakes; set aside. Immerse the tomatoes in a bowl of boiling water for 30 seconds, then remove with a slotted spoon and peel away their skins. Halve the tomatoes, deseed and chop the flesh.

3 Heat the olive oil in a large frying pan (large enough to hold and toss the spaghetti later). Add the chopped garlic and crushed chilli and cook over a medium high heat for 2 minutes; do not let the garlic brown. Stir in the chopped tomatoes and wine.

4 Add the clams in their shells to the pan. Season with salt and pepper, stir well and bring to the boil. Cover with a tight-fitting lid and cook for 2-3 minutes

to steam open the clams. Remove from the heat. Discard any clams which have not opened.

5 Meanwhile, cook the spaghetti in a large pan of boiling salted water until almost ready, but not quite *al dente* (about 1 minute less than the cooking time suggested on the packet). Drain thoroughly.

6 Return the clam sauce to the heat and stir in the parsley. Add the drained spaghetti and cook for 1 minute; the pasta should finish its cooking in the clam juices. Add the butter, toss lightly and serve at once.

VARIATIONS

When fresh clams are not available, use jars or cans in their shells, available from Italian delicatessens and larger supermarkets. Drain thoroughly before use, and include a few chopped anchovy fillets to taste.

Alternatively, replace the clams with 1 kg (2 lb) fresh mussels in their shells.

Chicken and Pasta Salad

PREPARATION TIME: 15 MINUTES + COOLING
COOKING TIME: 10 MINUTES
SERVES 4
300 CALORIES PER SERVING

175 g (6 oz) tricolour pasta spirals or shells

salt and pepper

15 ml (1 tbsp) olive oil

15 ml (1 level tbsp) pesto

1 garlic clove, skinned and crushed

6 spring onions, trimmed and sliced

1 bulb Florence fennel, trimmed and sliced

175 g (6 oz) cherry tomatoes, halved

8 pitted black olives, halved

125 g (4 oz) roast chicken

75 g (3 oz) cooked ham

30 ml (2 level tbsp) chopped mixed fresh herbs

15 ml (1 level tbsp) toasted pine nuts

1 Cook the pasta in boiling salted water for 8-10 minutes, or according to packet instructions, until just tender.

2 Meanwhile, gently heat the oil, pesto and garlic in a small saucepan. Drain the pasta and tip into a mixing bowl. Pour over the pesto mixture and toss well. Leave to cool.

3 Add the spring onions, fennel, cherry tomatoes and olives to the pasta. Cut the chicken and ham into strips. Add to the pasta, mix well, and season.

4 Turn into a serving bowl and sprinkle with the herbs and toasted pine nuts.

Rigatone with Artichokes in a Creamy Sauce

PREPARATION TIME: 10 MINUTES
COOKING TIME: 15 MINUTES
SERVES 4
660 CALORIES PER SERVING

---

150 g (5 oz) butter

---

75 g (3 oz) fresh white breadcrumbs

---

1 garlic clove, skinned and crushed

---

400 g (14 oz) dried rigatone

---

salt and pepper

---

grated rind of 1 lemon

---

284 ml (10 fl oz) carton of single cream

---

pinch of freshly grated nutmeg

---

250 g (9 oz) artichokes in oil, drained

---

30 ml (2 level tbsp) chopped fresh parsley

---

1 Melt 50 g (2 oz) of the butter in a frying pan, add the breadcrumbs and garlic, and fry until crisp and golden. Remove from the pan and set aside.

2 Cook the pasta in a large saucepan of boiling salted water for 10-12 minutes or until *al dente* (tender but still slightly firm).

3 Meanwhile, melt the remaining butter in a pan, add the lemon rind, and cook gently for a few seconds. Add the cream and season with salt, pepper and nutmeg. Bring to the boil and cook until reduced and thickened.

4 Cut the artichokes into quarters and stir them into the cream sauce. Keep the sauce warm.

5 Drain the pasta thoroughly and return to the saucepan. Add the lemon cream sauce, the artichokes and the parsley, and mix thoroughly. Serve at once, sprinkling each serving with the fried breadcrumbs.

Lasagnette with Pepperoni, Red Onion and Pimientos

PREPARATION TIME: 10 MINUTES
COOKING TIME: 20 MINUTES
SERVES 4
615 CALORIES PER SERVING

---

45 ml (3 tbsp) olive oil

---

2 red onions, skinned and sliced

---

3 garlic cloves, skinned and sliced

---

2 canned pimientos (red peppers), drained and cut into strips

---

125 g (4 oz) sliced pepperoni sausage

---

60 ml (4 tbsp) red wine

---

400 g (14 oz) can of chopped tomatoes

---

5 ml (1 level tsp) sun-dried tomato paste

---

salt and pepper

---

350 g (12 oz) dried lasagnette

---

75 ml (5 level tbsp) freshly grated Parmesan cheese

---

45 ml (3 level tbsp) chopped fresh parsley

---

1 Heat 30 ml (2 tbsp) of the oil in a large frying pan, add the onions and garlic, and cook for 5 minutes or until softened and golden. Add the pimiento strips, and continue to cook for a further minute. Remove the vegetables from the pan and set aside.

2 Heat the remaining oil in the pan, add the pepperoni, and cook over a high heat until browned and almost crisp. Return the vegetables to the pan and add the wine. Cook over a high heat until the wine is reduced by half. Add the tomatoes and tomato paste, and season with salt and pepper. Simmer for 15 minutes.

3 Meanwhile, cook the pasta in a large saucepan of boiling salted water for 10-12 minutes or until *al dente* (tender but still slightly firm). Drain the pasta thoroughly and return it to the saucepan. Add the vegetable and pepperoni sauce, and mix thoroughly. Add 30 ml (2 level tbsp) of the Parmesan cheese and all the parsley, and mix again. Serve at once, spinkled with the remaining Parmesan cheese.

Spaghetti with Garlic

PREPARATION TIME: 5 MINUTES
COOKING TIME: 10 MINUTES
SERVES 6
370 CALORIES PER SERVING

---

450 g (1 lb) dried spaghetti

---

salt and pepper

---

75 ml (5 tbsp) virgin olive oil

---

2 garlic cloves, skinned and crushed

---

1 fresh chilli, deseeded and chopped

---

30 ml (2 level tbsp) chopped fresh parsley, coriander or basil (optional)

---

1 Cook the spaghetti in boiling salted water for 8-10 minutes or until *al dente* (tender but still firm to the bite).

2 Meanwhile, heat the oil in a heavy-based saucepan, add the garlic and chilli, and fry for 3-4 minutes, stirring occasionally. Do not allow the garlic and chilli to become too brown or the oil will taste bitter. Remove from the heat and set aside until the pasta is cooked.

3 Drain the pasta thoroughly. Reheat the oil over a very high heat for 1 minute, then pour over the pasta with the herbs, if using. Season with salt and pepper and serve immediately.

Spaghetti with Aubergine and Mozzarella

PREPARATION TIME: 10 MINUTES
COOKING TIME: 20 MINUTES
SERVES 4
745 CALORIES PER SERVING

90 ml (3 fl oz) olive oil

1 onion, chopped

2 garlic cloves, skinned and crushed

1 medium aubergine, about 400 g (14 oz), cut into small chunks

400 g (14 oz) can of chopped tomatoes

salt and pepper

350 g (12 oz) dried spaghetti

30 ml (2 level tbsp) capers in wine vinegar, drained

15 g (½ oz) fresh basil leaves, shredded

150 g (5 oz) Mozzarella, diced

30 ml (2 level tbsp) pine nuts

60 ml (4 level tbsp) freshly grated Parmesan cheese

1 Heat half the oil in a frying pan, add the onion, garlic and aubergine, and sauté for 8-10 minutes. Add the tomatoes, season with salt and pepper and simmer for 15 minutes.

2 Meanwhile, cook the pasta in a large saucepan of boiling salted water for 10-12 minutes or until *al dente* (tender but still slightly firm). Drain well, return to the pan, and stir in the tomato and aubergine mixture. Add the capers, basil, Mozzarella and pine nuts, and mix well. Check the seasoning, and serve at once, with the grated Parmesan cheese.

Pasta with Pan-fried Salmon

PREPARATION TIME: 10 MINUTES
COOKING TIME: 20 MINUTES
SERVES 4
340 CALORIES PER SERVING

---

275 g (10 oz) skinned salmon fillet

---

15 ml (1 tbsp) oil

---

125 g (4 oz) dried pasta shapes

---

salt and pepper

---

15 ml (1 level tbsp) plain flour

---

300 ml (½ pint) skimmed milk

---

30 ml (2 level tbsp) chopped fresh parsley

---

30 ml (2 level tbsp) capers

---

50 g (2 oz) can of anchovy fillets, drained

---

1 garlic clove, skinned and crushed

---

5 ml (1 level tsp) Dijon mustard

---

15 ml (1 tbsp) lemon juice

---

flat-leaf parsley, to garnish

---

1 Cut the salmon into thick slices. Heat the oil in a non-stick frying pan and fry the salmon for 5-7 minutes, turning once.

2 Meanwhile, cook the pasta in a large saucepan of boiling salted water for 10-12 minutes or until *al dente* (tender but still slightly firm).

3 Mix the flour to a paste with a little of the milk. Place in a saucepan with the remaining milk, 150 ml (¼ pint) water and the parsley, capers, anchovies, garlic, mustard and lemon juice. Bring slowly to the boil, stirring, then reduce the heat and simmer for 2-3 minutes. Season with salt and pepper, adding only a little salt as anchovies are salty.

4 Serve the salmon on a bed of pasta. Spoon the sauce over and garnish.

Spinach Tagliatelle with Blue Cheese

PREPARATION TIME: 5 MINUTES
COOKING TIME: 2-12 MINUTES
SERVES 4
695 CALORIES PER SERVING

400 g (14 oz) fresh or dried spinach tagliatelle
salt and pepper
150 g (5 oz) ricotta cheese
150 g (5 oz) vegetarian blue Stilton cheese
150 g (5 oz) crème fraîche
4-6 spring onions, trimmed and finely chopped
15 ml (1 level tbsp) chopped fresh coriander leaves
coriander sprigs, to garnish

1 Cook the tagliatelle in a large pan of boiling salted water, until *al dente* (tender but still firm to the bite). Fresh pasta will only take 2-3 minutes to cook; for dried pasta, refer to the packet instructions.

2 While the pasta is cooking, crumble the ricotta and Stilton cheeses together into a bowl. Add the crème fraîche and stir to mix well.

3 Drain the pasta thoroughly in a colander and turn into a heated serving dish. Immediately add the crumbled cheese mixture, spring onions and coriander. Season with salt and pepper. Using two forks, lift the tagliatelle to coat with the sauce. Garnish with sprigs of coriander and serve immediately.

VARIATION

Replace the spring onions with 225 g (8 oz) leeks. Clean the leeks thoroughly, then slice. Sauté in a little olive oil until softened. Add to the pasta with the crumbled cheese mixture and toss well.

Pasta and Mushrooms Baked with Two Cheeses

PREPARATION TIME: 5 MINUTES
COOKING TIME: 25 MINUTES
SERVES 2-3
955-630 CALORIES PER SERVING

225 g (8 oz) dried tagliatelle or other noodles

salt and pepper

25 g (1 oz) butter

1 garlic clove, skinned and crushed

225 g (8 oz) mushrooms, wiped and thinly sliced

50 g (2 oz) Stilton cheese

60 ml (4 level tbsp) double cream

1 egg, lightly beaten

125 g (4 oz) Mozzarella cheese, grated

1 Cook the pasta in boiling salted water for 10-12 minutes or until just tender. Drain well.

2 Meanwhile, melt the butter in a large frying pan and cook the garlic and mushrooms, stirring frequently, until just softened.

3 Crumble in the Stilton cheese and cook for 1-2 minutes, stirring continuously. Stir in the cream, and season with salt and pepper.

4 Season the pasta with plenty of pepper. Mix into the mushroom sauce. Stir in the egg, and mix together thoroughly.

5 Place the mixture in a buttered ovenproof serving dish and sprinkle the Mozzarella on top. Cover with foil and bake in the oven at 180°C (350°F) mark 4 for 10 minutes, then remove the foil and bake at 220°C (425°F) mark 7 for a further 10-15 minutes or until brown and crusty on top. Serve immediately.

Pad Thai Noodles

PREPARATION TIME: 15 MINUTES
COOKING TIME: 5 MINUTES
SERVES 4
615 CALORIES PER SERVING

250 g (9 oz) flat, thin rice or egg noodles
30 ml (2 tbsp) oil
125 g (4 oz) turnip, peeled and diced
2 garlic cloves, skinned and crushed
2.5 ml (½ level tsp) hot paprika
60-75 ml (4-5 tbsp) Thai-style fish sauce
juice of 1 lime
15 ml (1 level tbsp) tomato purée
125 g (4 oz) tofu, diced
50 g (2 oz) roasted peanuts, finely chopped
125 g (4 oz) cooked peeled prawns
175 g (6 oz) beansprouts
2 eggs, beaten
chopped peanuts, to serve
whole cooked prawns and basil, to garnish

1 Cook the noodles according to packet instructions.

2 Heat the oil in a wok or large, non-stick sauté pan. Add the noodles, turnip, garlic and paprika, and sauté for 1-2 minutes, stirring to prevent the noodles sticking. Add the fish sauce, lime juice and tomato purée and cook for a further 1 minute, stirring continuously.

3 Stir in the tofu, peanuts, prawns and beansprouts. Lower the heat, add the eggs and stir for about 1 minute or until the noodles are coated in lightly cooked egg. Sprinkle with chopped peanuts and garnish with prawns and basil.

Stir-fried Noodles with Shredded Green Vegetables

PREPARATION TIME: 15 MINUTES
COOKING TIME: 10 MINUTES
SERVES 4
300 CALORIES PER SERVING

salt and pepper
175 g (6 oz) dried egg thread noodles
45 ml (3 tbsp) oil
4 spring onions, trimmed, quartered and cut into thin shreds
1 courgette, trimmed, quartered and cut into thin shreds
½ green pepper, deseeded, quartered and cut into thin shreds
2 celery sticks, trimmed, quartered and cut into thin shreds
75 g (3 oz) spinach, finely shredded
2.5 cm (1 inch) piece of fresh root ginger, peeled and chopped
1 garlic clove, skinned and crushed
1 chicken stock cube, crumbled
15 ml (1 tbsp) hoisin sauce
celery leaves, to garnish

1 Bring a large pan of salted water to the boil, add the noodles, remove from the heat and leave to soak for 4 minutes. Drain well.

2 Heat 30 ml (2 tbsp) oil in a wok or large frying pan. Add the vegetables, ginger and garlic, and stir-fry for 2 minutes.

3 Add the remaining oil to the pan, then add the noodles and stir-fry for 2 minutes. Sprinkle the crumbled stock cube, hoisin sauce and 15 ml (1 tbsp) water on top and cook for 2 minutes, lifting and mixing the noodles using two forks. Season with pepper and serve immediately with garnish.

Seafood Noodles

PREPARATION TIME: 15 MINUTES
COOKING TIME: 10 MINUTES
SERVES 4
460 CALORIES PER SERVING

salt

225 g (8 oz) Chinese egg noodles

5 ml (1 tsp) sesame oil

45 ml (3 tbsp) groundnut or vegetable oil

6 spring onions, trimmed and thinly sliced

1 onion, skinned, halved and finely shredded

2 celery sticks, trimmed and thinly sliced diagonally

6 baby sweetcorn, washed and halved

125 g (4 oz) young spinach leaves, shredded

227 g (8 oz) pack of ready-cooked seafood cocktail
(see page 133)

45 ml (3 tbsp) light soy sauce

30 ml (2 tbsp) orange juice

30 ml (2 tbsp) dry sherry

30 ml (2 tbsp) oyster sauce

1 Bring a large saucepan of salted water to the boil, add the noodles and remove the pan from the heat. Leave to soak for 6 minutes, then drain well and toss in the sesame oil.

2 Heat the groundnut oil in a wok or large frying pan. Add the onions, celery and sweetcorn, and stir-fry for 3 minutes. Stir in the shredded spinach leaves and stir-fry for 1 minute.

3 Add the noodles and seafood, and toss well together, then add the remaining ingredients and cook for 2-3 minutes, tossing and mixing lightly.

4 Transfer the mixture to a hot serving dish and serve immediately.

Noodles with Fried Eggs

PREPARATION TIME: 5 MINUTES
COOKING TIME: 10 MINUTES
SERVES 2
670 CALORIES PER SERVING

125-175 g (4-6 oz) buckwheat noodles (see Note)

salt

30 ml (2 tbsp) sesame oil

1 onion, skinned and sliced

1 large carrot, peeled and very thinly sliced

1 small garlic clove, skinned and crushed

about 3 large Chinese leaves or a handful of spinach leaves, roughly chopped

45 ml (3 tbsp) light soy sauce

5 ml (1 level tsp) sugar

15 ml (1 tbsp) white wine vinegar

vegetable oil for frying

2 eggs

1 Cook the noodles in boiling salted water according to packet instructions.

2 Meanwhile, heat the sesame oil in a large frying pan. Add the onion, carrot and garlic and fry over a very high heat until tinged with brown and softened, stirring all the time. Add the Chinese leaves or spinach and the soy sauce, sugar and vinegar, reduce the heat and simmer very gently.

3 Heat a little oil in a frying pan and fry the eggs. Meanwhile, drain the noodles and stir into the vegetable mixture, tossing everything together. Divide the noodles between two plates and top each portion with an egg. Serve at once.

NOTE

Buckwheat noodles are sold in many health food shops, some supermarkets and Japanese food shops. If unavailable, use thin egg noodles instead.

Egg Noodles with Chicken and Vegetables

PREPARATION TIME: 10 MINUTES
COOKING TIME: ABOUT 10 MINUTES
SERVES 2
730 CALORIES PER SERVING

250 g (8.8 oz) packet of thin egg noodles

about 30 ml (2 tbsp) vegetable oil

1 skinless chicken breast fillet, cut into very thin strips

2.5 cm (1 inch) piece of fresh root ginger, peeled and finely
chopped (optional)

1 garlic clove, skinned and finely chopped

1 red pepper, deseeded and cut into thin strips

4 spring onions, trimmed and cut into thin strips

2 carrots, peeled and cut into thin strips

125 g (4 oz) shiitake or button mushrooms, wiped and halved

a few beansprouts (optional)

45 ml (3 tbsp) hoisin sauce

30 ml (2 tbsp) light soy sauce

15 ml (1 tbsp) chilli sauce

shredded spring onions and sesame seeds, to garnish

1 Bring a large saucepan of water to the boil. Add the noodles and cook for
2-3 minutes or according to packet instructions. Drain thoroughly and toss
with a little of the oil to prevent them sticking together. Set aside.

2 Heat the remaining oil in a wok or large frying pan. Add the chicken, ginger
and garlic, and cook over a very high heat until the chicken is browned on
the outside and cooked right through.

3 Add all the vegetables to the wok or frying pan and stir-fry over a high heat
for a few minutes or until they are just cooked, but still crunchy.

4 Add the hoisin sauce, soy sauce and chilli sauce, and stir to mix. Add the noodles and cook for 1-2 minutes to heat through. Serve immediately, sprinkled with shredded spring onion and a few sesame seeds.

VARIATION

Replace the chicken with thinly sliced turkey escalopes. Increase the heat of the dish by frying a chopped chilli with the onion and ginger.

Quick Pasta Ideas

For an extra-quick supper, it's hard to beat a plate of pasta. Here are some ideas for 30-minute pasta suppers. For four servings, cook 350 g (12 oz) dried pasta in boiling salted water for 10-12 minutes or until al dente (tender but still slightly firm). Drain and mix with one of the following:

✦ Mix 175 g (6 oz) roughly chopped softish blue cheese, such as dolcelatte or cambozola, or a low-fat soft cheese with garlic and herbs, such as Boursin, with a handful of chopped toasted walnuts and 200 ml (7 fl oz) single cream. Season with plenty of black pepper. Heat with the cooked pasta for 1-2 minutes, then serve immediately. Stir in a little chopped fresh rosemary if wished.

✦ Stir 225 g (8 oz) diced Mozzarella cheese into 450 g (1 lb) chopped fresh tomatoes with the grated rind of 1 lemon, 45 ml (3 tbsp) balsamic vinegar and plenty of chopped fresh basil. Heat with the cooked pasta for 1 minute, then serve.

✦ Mix 350 g (12 oz) blanched seasonal vegetables (courgettes, asparagus, etc.) with 50 g (2 oz) chopped ham, 150 ml (¼ pint) crème fraîche and 50 g (2 oz) freshly grated Gruyère cheese. Stir into the cooked pasta with a few chopped chives if wished.

✦ Beat a little milk into soft cheese with garlic and herbs; toss into spaghetti with crispy bacon and cooked broccoli.

✦ Cook a handful of chopped pine nuts or walnuts in butter. Add 15 ml (1 level tbsp) chopped fresh marjoram and heat through. Toss with cooked pasta, plenty of grated Parmesan and black pepper.

✦ Pan-fry 225 g (8 oz) chicken livers with a couple of slices of chopped pancetta or bacon and 1-2 crushed garlic cloves. Add a splash of balsamic or red wine vinegar. Toss with hot pasta.

✦ Heat a can of chopped tomatoes with a splash of red wine, garlic, lots of chopped chillies, a bay leaf and plenty of fresh basil. Add a couple of chopped sun-dried tomatoes if you have them. Boil until well reduced. Season with plenty of salt and pepper. Toss with hot pasta or add chunks of cooked spicy sausage or drained canned clams, if liked. For a richer, creamier result, blend the sauce above with mascarpone.

✦ Stir-fry 2 sliced courgettes with a large pinch of cumin seeds and half a bunch of chopped spring onions. Add 60 ml (4 tbsp) hummus, thinned with a little milk, stock or water, and simmer to heat through. Season with pepper.

✦ Sauté mushrooms with garlic, a bay leaf and a sprig of thyme or rosemary. Add a little stock, white wine or water to moisten and bubble to reduce. Add cream or crème fraîche and plenty of salt and pepper.

✦ Fry 275 g (10 oz) chopped, smoked bacon until crispy with one small, chopped red chilli, in about 45 ml (3 tbsp) oil. Stir in 450 g (1 lb) halved, ripe cherry tomatoes and about 60 ml (4 level tbsp) chopped fresh parsley and thyme. Season with plenty of black pepper. Heat with the cooked pasta for 1-2 minutes, then serve.

Vegetarian Dishes

Courgette and Pesto 'Pizzas'

PREPARATION TIME: 20 MINUTES
COOKING TIME: 10 MINUTES
SERVES 6
90 CALORIES PER SERVING

---

225 g (8 oz) courgettes

---

olive oil

---

2 beefsteak tomatoes, about 450 g (1 lb) total weight

---

30 ml (2 level tbsp) red pesto sauce or tapenade (olive paste)

---

a large handful of fresh basil leaves

---

salt and pepper

---

50 g (2 oz) Parmesan cheese

---

garlic bread, to serve

---

1 Cut the courgettes diagonally into slices about 5 mm (¼ inch) thick. Lightly brush a non-stick frying pan with oil. Cook the courgette slices on both sides for about 5 minutes or until brown and tender.

2 Cut each tomato into three slices about 1 cm (½ inch) thick and place on a lightly oiled baking sheet. Spread 5 ml (1 level tsp) pesto or tapenade on top of each slice. Place five or six basil leaves in a circle on top of the pesto.

3 Place an overlapping circle of courgettes on the basil leaves. Season with salt and pepper.

4 Cook in the oven at 200°C (400°F) mark 6 for 10 minutes. Top with thinly pared Parmesan cheese (see Cook's Tip). Serve immediately, accompanied by garlic bread.

COOK'S TIP

To pare fresh Parmesan cheese, use a swivel-bladed vegetable peeler.

Curried Tofu Burgers

PREPARATION TIME: 20 MINUTES
COOKING TIME: 6-8 MINUTES
SERVES 4
230 CALORIES PER SERVING

15 ml (1 tbsp) oil

1 large carrot, peeled and finely grated

1 large onion, peeled and finely grated

10 ml (2 level tsp) coriander seeds, finely crushed (optional)

1 garlic clove, skinned and crushed

5 ml (1 level tsp) curry paste

5 ml (1 level tsp) tomato purée

225 g (8 oz) packet of tofu

25 g (1 oz) fresh wholemeal breadcrumbs

25 g (1 oz) mixed nuts, finely chopped

salt and pepper

plain flour for coating

oil for frying or grilling

1 Heat the 15 ml (1 tbsp) oil in a large frying pan. Add the carrot and onion and fry for 3-4 minutes or until the vegetables are softened, stirring all the time. Add the coriander seeds, if using, the garlic, curry paste and tomato purée. Increase the heat and cook for 2 minutes, stirring all the time.

2 Mash the tofu with a potato masher, then stir into the vegetables with the breadcrumbs and nuts. Season with salt and pepper, and beat thoroughly until the mixture starts to stick together. With floured hands, shape the mixture into eight burgers.

3 Heat some oil in a frying pan and fry the burgers for 3-4 minutes on each side or until golden brown. Alternatively, brush lightly with oil and cook under a hot grill for about 3 minutes on each side or until golden brown. Drain on absorbent kitchen paper and serve hot.

Glazed Vegetable Pastries

PREPARATION TIME: 15 MINUTES
COOKING TIME: ABOUT 10 MINUTES
SERVES 4 OR 8
250 CALORIES PER PASTRY

24 filo pastry squares, each 10 x 10 cm (4 x 4 inches)

40 g (1½ oz) butter, melted

500 g (1 lb 2 oz) mixed baby vegetables, such as carrots, corn cobs, courgettes and mangetout

salt and pepper

90 ml (6 tbsp) mayonnaise

15-30 ml (1-2 level tbsp) chopped mixed fresh herbs, such as chives, parsley and chervil

75 g (3 oz) fresh soft goat's cheese

a little single cream

1 Layer the filo pastry squares over a buttered upturned Yorkshire pudding tin, brushing liberally with melted butter, to make four baskets. Bake in the oven at 190°C (375°F) mark 5 for 7-8 minutes or until crisp and golden. Carefully lift each pastry basket off the tin and place on a wire rack.

2 Meanwhile, steam or cook the vegetables in boiling salted water until just tender. Drain well.

3 In a bowl, beat the mayonnaise with the herbs and goat's cheese until evenly blended. Add enough cream to give a coating consistency and season with salt and pepper.

4 Place the pastry cases on a baking sheet and divide the vegetables between them. Spoon the cheese mixture over the vegetables. Protect the filo edges with foil and place under a hot grill for about 30 seconds to glaze the vegetables. Serve immediately.

Vegetable Kebabs with Tofu Sauce

PREPARATION TIME: 15 MINUTES
COOKING TIME: 10 MINUTES
SERVES 2-4
480-240 CALORIES PER SERVING

300 g (10 oz) silken tofu

30 ml (2 tbsp) olive oil

20 ml (4 tsp) soy sauce

about 30 ml (2 tbsp) lemon juice

1-2 garlic cloves, crushed

15 ml (1 tbsp) sesame oil (optional)

salt and pepper

4 small courgettes

6 baby corn cobs

16 button mushrooms

12 cherry tomatoes or 3 medium tomatoes, quartered

12 bay leaves

30 ml (2 level tbsp) sesame seeds

1 Put the tofu in a blender or food processor with 15 ml (1 tbsp) oil, 10 ml (2 tsp) soy sauce, the lemon juice, garlic and sesame oil, if using. Work until evenly combined, then add salt and pepper to taste and more lemon juice, if liked. Pour into a jug and chill.

2 Cut each courgette into three chunks. Blanch in boiling salted water for 1 minute, then drain. Halve the corn cobs diagonally. Thread the vegetables and bay leaves alternately on to oiled skewers.

3 Mix the remaining oil and soy sauce with the sesame seeds. Brush over the kebabs and grill for about 10 minutes, turning and brushing frequently. Serve hot, on a bed of boiled rice, with the tofu sauce handed separately.

Vegetable Couscous

PREPARATION TIME: 20 MINUTES
SERVES 8
370 CALORIES PER SERVING

350 g (12 oz) couscous
225 g (8 oz) broccoli
125 g (4 oz) mangetout
225 g (8 oz) fennel
salt and pepper
125 g (4 oz) petits pois
2 lemons
175 ml (6 fl oz) olive oil
60 ml (4 level tbsp) wholegrain mustard
30 ml (2 tbsp) runny honey
1 bunch of spring onions, trimmed and chopped
1 bunch of chives, chopped

1 Place the couscous in a bowl and pour over 600 ml (1 pint) boiling water. Cover with foil and leave to stand for about 10 minutes or until all the water is absorbed.

2 Meanwhile, cut the broccoli into small florets, and top and tail the mangetout. Trim, halve and slice the fennel. Blanch in boiling salted water with the petits pois for about 2 minutes.

3 Meanwhile, grate the rind of 1 lemon and whisk together with 75 ml (5 tbsp) lemon juice, the oil, wholegrain mustard, honey and seasoning. Whisk the onions and chives into the dressing.

4 Drain the vegetables and fold into the warm couscous with the dressing. Serve immediately.

Vegetable and Apple Stir-fry

PREPARATION TIME: 15 MINUTES
COOKING TIME: 15 MINUTES
SERVES 4
285 CALORIES PER SERVING

60 ml (4 tbsp) oil
1 garlic clove, skinned and crushed
350 g (12 oz) small trimmed leeks, sliced
4 green celery sticks, trimmed and sliced
225 g (8 oz) courgettes, sliced
1 red pepper, deseeded and chopped
30 ml (2 level tbsp) medium curry paste
5 ml (1 level tsp) ground ginger
15 ml (1 tbsp) runny honey
2 crisp, green eating apples, cored and roughly chopped
50 g (2 oz) unsalted cashew nuts
salt and pepper
juice of 1 lemon
flat-leaf parsley, to garnish

1 Heat the oil in a non-stick sauté pan, add the garlic, and cook for a few seconds. Stir in the vegetables and cook over a high heat for 10 minutes, stirring occasionally.

2 Add the curry paste, ginger, honey and 45 ml (3 tbsp) water, and stir until smooth.

3 Add the apples to the pan with the cashew nuts and plenty of salt and pepper. Cook for a further 5 minutes or until the vegetables are just tender. Squeeze lemon juice over to serve. Garnish with flat-leaf parsley.

Aubergines with Mustard Seeds and Yogurt

PREPARATION TIME: 5 MINUTES
COOKING TIME: 20 MINUTES
SERVES 4-6
210-140 CALORIES PER SERVING

Grilling whole aubergines until the skins char gives them a wonderful smoky flavour. Serve as a main meal with pilau rice.

3 medium aubergines, about 900 g (2 lb) total weight
60 ml (4 tbsp) oil
30 ml (2 level tbsp) black mustard seeds, ground
2.5 ml (½ level tsp) chilli powder
60 ml (4 level tbsp) chopped fresh coriander
5 ml (1 level tsp) salt
300 ml (½ pint) natural yogurt

1 Put the aubergines under a preheated grill for about 15 minutes, turning occasionally. The skins should be black and charred and the flesh soft.

2 Leave the aubergines until just cool enough to handle, then peel the skins off and discard. Chop the flesh roughly.

3 Heat the oil in a heavy-based frying pan and add the ground mustard seeds, chopped aubergine flesh and chilli powder. Stir over a moderate heat for about 5 minutes or until thoroughly hot, then add the coriander.

4 Beat the salt into the yogurt, then stir into the aubergine until evenly blended. Turn into a warmed serving dish and serve immediately.

Winter Vegetables with Lentils and Ginger

PREPARATION TIME: 15 MINUTES
COOKING TIME: 16 MINUTES
SERVES 4
290 CALORIES PER SERVING

45 ml (3 tbsp) olive oil

5 ml (1 level tsp) ground cumin

15 ml (1 level tbsp) ground coriander

15 ml (1 level tbsp) mustard powder

1 garlic clove, skinned and crushed

1 cm (½ inch) piece of fresh root ginger, peeled and chopped

225 g (8 oz) baby onions, skinned

225 g (8 oz) button mushrooms, wiped

225 g (8 oz) carrots, scrubbed and thinly sliced

225 g (8 oz) trimmed leeks, thickly sliced and washed

275 g (10 oz) parsnips, peeled and diced

175 g (6 oz) split red lentils, boiled rapidly for 10 minutes, then drained

900 ml (1½ pints) vegetable stock

chopped fresh coriander

salt and pepper

1 Heat the oil in a large saucepan, add the ground cumin, ground coriander, mustard, garlic and ginger, and sauté, stirring, for 1 minute. Mix in the vegetables, lentils and stock. Bring to the boil, then reduce the heat, cover and simmer for 15 minutes or until the lentils are just tender.

2 Stir in fresh coriander and adjust the seasoning. Serve hot with brown rice, garnished with sprigs of coriander.

Spicy Vegetable and Bean Tacos

PREPARATION TIME: 10 MINUTES
COOKING TIME: 25 MINUTES
SERVES 3
395 CALORIES PER SERVING

15 ml (1 tbsp) olive oil

1 onion, skinned and chopped

1 garlic clove, skinned and finely chopped

1 red pepper, deseeded and diced

1 green pepper, deseeded and diced

5 ml (1 level tsp) ground cumin

5 ml (1 level tsp) paprika

5 ml (1 level tsp) ground coriander

430 g (15 oz) can of red kidney beans, drained and rinsed

227 g (8 oz) can of chopped tomatoes

salt and pepper

chopped fresh coriander, to garnish

3-6 Mexican taco shells

To serve

75 g (3 oz) low-fat Cheddar-type cheese, grated

black olives

pickled chillies

1 Heat the oil in a non-stick saucepan, add the onion and garlic, and cook for about 5 minutes or until softened. Add the peppers and cook, stirring frequently, for a further 5 minutes or until softened.

2 Stir in the spices and cook, stirring, for 1 minute. Stir in the kidney beans and tomatoes with their juice and simmer for about 15 minutes or until thickened. Season with salt and pepper.

3 Meanwhile, heat the taco shells according to the packet instructions. To serve, put the cheese, olives, chillies and vegetable filling in bowls, garnish with coriander, and serve with the warmed tacos.

Savoury Nut Burgers

PREPARATION TIME: 20 MINUTES
COOKING TIME: 8 MINUTES
SERVES 8
300 CALORIES PER SERVING

25 g (1 oz) butter or margarine
1 large onion, skinned and chopped
15 ml (1 level tbsp) chopped fresh parsley
30 ml (2 level tbsp) plain wholemeal flour
150 ml (¼ pint) milk
225 g (8 oz) chopped mixed nuts
15 ml (1 tbsp) soy sauce
15 ml (1 level tbsp) tomato purée
175 g (6 oz) fresh wholemeal breadcrumbs
1 egg, beaten
pepper

1 Melt the butter in a saucepan and lightly fry the onion and parsley until soft. Stir in the flour and cook for 2 minutes. Remove from the heat and gradually stir in the milk. Bring to the boil, stirring, until the sauce is thickened and smooth. Simmer for 1-2 minutes.

2 Add the nuts, soy sauce, tomato purée, breadcrumbs, egg and pepper to taste. Mix well.

3 Divide into eight portions and shape into burgers. Cook under a hot grill for 4 minutes on each side. Serve hot.

Tomato and Garlic Pizza

PREPARATION TIME: 15 MINUTES
COOKING TIME: 20 MINUTES
SERVES 2
485 CALORIES PER SERVING

---

1 medium garlic bulb

---

olive oil for basting

---

4 medium tomatoes, about 400 g (14 oz) total weight

---

salt and pepper

---

145 g (5.1 oz) packet of pizza-base mix

---

15 ml (1 level tbsp) chopped fresh rosemary or 10 ml
(2 level tsp) dried rosemary

---

75 g (3 oz) feta cheese

---

about 8 black olives

---

about 8 fresh basil leaves

---

1 Divide the garlic into cloves, discarding the outer, papery layers, but leaving the inner skins intact. Toss in a little oil.

2 Meanwhile, roughly chop the tomatoes and place in a bowl with 5 ml (1 tsp) salt. Mix well.

3 Make up the pizza-base mix according to the packet instructions. As you are kneading the dough, knead in the rosemary until it is evenly incorporated.

4 Roll out the dough thinly to a 25 cm (10 inch) round on a lightly floured surface. Transfer to a lightly greased and floured baking sheet.

5 Spoon the tomatoes over the pizza base to within 1 cm (½ inch) of the edge, and crumble the feta cheese on top. Scatter the olives, garlic cloves and basil over the top. Season with pepper only.

6 Bake in the oven at 220°C (425°F) mark 7 for 20 minutes or until the base is crisp and golden. Serve immediately.

Tomato Risotto

PREPARATION TIME: 10 MINUTES
COOKING TIME: 15 MINUTES
SERVES 6
275 CALORIES PER SERVING

30 ml (2 tbsp) olive oil

125 g (4 oz) onion, skinned and finely chopped

350 g (12 oz) Arborio (risotto) rice

pinch of saffron strands (optional)

salt and pepper

60 ml (4 tbsp) dry white wine

750 ml (1¼ pints) vegetable stock

275 g (10 oz) yellow cherry tomatoes, halved

1 large sprig of fresh rosemary, roughly chopped

1 Heat the oil in a flameproof casserole, add the onion and cook for 2-3 minutes or until beginning to soften. Stir in the rice and saffron, if using. Season well with salt and pepper and pour in the wine and stock, stirring well to mix.

2 Bring to the boil, stirring, then cover and simmer the risotto for 5 minutes. Stir in the tomatoes and rosemary. Re-cover and simmer for a further 5-7 minutes or until the rice is tender and most of the liquid absorbed. Season and serve.

VARIATIONS

✦ Replace the tomatoes with 225 g (8 oz) asparagus tips.

✦ Replace the tomatoes with 450 g (1 lb) fresh peas, shelled (or about 225 g (8 oz) frozen petits pois, thawed).

✦ Omit the tomatoes. Sauté 450 g (1 lb) mixed mushrooms with the oil in step 2.

Mushroom and Parmesan Risotto

PREPARATION TIME: 15 MINUTES
COOKING TIME: 20 MINUTES
SERVES 4
420 CALORIES PER SERVING

225 g (8 oz) broccoli florets

175 g (6 oz) French beans

salt and pepper

30 ml (2 tbsp) olive oil

1 medium onion, skinned and finely chopped

350 g (12 oz) Arborio (risotto) or long-grain white rice (see Cook's Tip)

pinch of saffron strands (optional)

60 ml (4 tbsp) dry white wine

pared rind and juice of 1 lemon

750 ml (1¼ pints) vegetable stock

175 g (6 oz) flat mushrooms, wiped and sliced

finely pared Parmesan cheese, to serve

1 Break the broccoli into very small florets. Top and tail the French beans and cut in half lengthways. Blanch the broccoli and beans together in boiling salted water for 3-4 minutes. Drain and refresh under cold running water.

2 Heat the oil in a heavy-based saucepan or flameproof casserole, and cook the onion gently for 2-3 minutes or until beginning to soften. Stir in the rice and saffron, if using. Season well and pour in the wine. Add the pared lemon rind, 30 ml (2 tbsp) lemon juice and the stock. Bring to the boil, stirring.

3 Cover the risotto and simmer for 5 minutes. Stir in the mushrooms, broccoli and French beans. Re-cover and simmer for a further 5 minutes, or until the rice is tender and most of the liquid is absorbed.

4 Discard the lemon rind and transfer the risotto to warmed serving plates. Top with slivers of Parmesan cheese and serve at once.

COOK'S TIP

If you use Arborio rice, add a little more stock and cook for 1-2 minutes longer.

Stuffed Mushrooms

PREPARATION TIME: 10 MINUTES
COOKING TIME: 15-20 MINUTES
SERVES 4
340 CALORIES PER SERVING

8 flat mushrooms, peeled and stalks removed

60 ml (4 tbsp) olive oil

125 g (4 oz) mascarpone cheese

1 garlic clove, skinned and crushed

4-6 spring onions, trimmed and finely chopped

6 black olives, pitted and chopped

½ large red pepper, deseeded and finely diced

45 ml (3 level tbsp) chopped fresh parsley

salt and pepper

30 ml (2 level tbsp) freshly grated Parmesan cheese

tomato strips and flat-leaf parsley sprigs, to garnish

1 Brush the mushrooms with olive oil and arrange, flat sides up, in a baking dish. Mix together the cheese, garlic, spring onions, black olives, red pepper and parsley. Season with salt and pepper.

2 Spoon the filling on to the mushrooms, then drizzle with more olive oil and sprinkle with the Parmesan cheese. Bake in the oven at 190°C (375°F) mark 5 for 15-20 minutes or until the mushrooms are tender. Serve hot, garnished with tomato strips and flat-leaf parsley sprigs.

Spinach and Lentil Roulade

PREPARATION TIME: 10 MINUTES
COOKING TIME: 20 MINUTES
SERVES 4
430 CALORIES PER SERVING

75 g (3 oz) butter or margarine
125 g (4 oz) frozen chopped spinach, thawed and thoroughly drained
50 g (2 oz) plain flour
300 ml (½ pint) milk
2 eggs, separated
175 g (6 oz) split red lentils, rinsed
50 g (2 oz) spring onions, trimmed and chopped
salt and pepper
30 ml (2 level tbsp) tomato ketchup
15 ml (1 level tbsp) creamed horseradish

1 Grease and line a 33 x 23 cm (13 x 9 inch) Swiss roll tin with non-stick baking parchment.

2 Melt 50 g (2 oz) butter in a saucepan and stir in the spinach and flour. Cook for 1 minute, then add the milk. Bring to the boil, stirring, and simmer for 2-3 minutes. Remove from the heat and beat in the egg yolks. Stiffly whisk the egg whites and fold into the mixture. Spoon into the prepared tin and spread evenly. Bake in the oven at 220°C (425°F) mark 7 for about 15 minutes or until well risen and firm to the touch.

3 Meanwhile, cook the lentils and spring onions in boiling salted water for 15-20 minutes or until tender. Drain well, then beat in the tomato ketchup, horseradish and remaining butter. Season with salt and pepper.

4 Turn out the roulade on to a sheet of non-stick baking parchment and peel off the lining paper. Spread the lentil mixture over the surface and roll up like a Swiss roll, using the paper to help. Serve immediately.

COOK'S TIP

Make sure that the spinach is really thoroughly drained before adding it to the sauce. It's a good idea to wrap it in a double thickness of muslin or a clean tea towel and to wring it out over the sink to remove all traces of water.

Quick Vegetarian Suppers

Easy to make at the last minute, these quick supper ideas are complete meals.

✦ Sauté chopped onions, garlic and plenty of fresh ginger in a little oil until softened. Add a little curry paste, canned chopped tomatoes and drained and rinsed canned chick-peas. Simmer until the tomatoes are well reduced. Add fresh coriander if available. Serve with rice and yogurt.

✦ Toss chunks of courgette and green, red and yellow peppers with virgin olive oil and sliced garlic. Roast in a very hot oven for about 20 minutes or until softened. Serve with slices of grilled halloumi cheese.

✦ Stir cooked broad beans (fresh or frozen), chunks of feta cheese (check the packaging for vegetarian brands) and blanched green beans through cooked rice. Moisten with garlic vinaigrette. Serve warm.

✦ Make potato fritters with 350 g (12 oz) leftover or freshly made mashed potato. Add enough beaten egg to bind and flavour with chopped spring onion and pickled chillies if liked. Add a handful of grated Parmesan or Cheddar cheese and plenty of seasoning. Shape into patties and coat with sesame seeds, breadcrumbs or cornmeal. Fry in butter and oil until browned on both sides. Serve with chutney and salad.

✦ Dip aubergine slices in batter and deep-fry. Serve with lemon wedges, tzatziki or hummus and olives.

✦ A little chopped blue cheese melted into crème fraîche makes a delicious sauce for pasta, or you can pour it over broccoli or cauliflower just before serving.

Side Dishes and Salads

Crispy 'Seaweed'

PREPARATION TIME: 10 MINUTES
COOKING TIME: 5 MINUTES
SERVES 4
380 CALORIES PER SERVING

---

700 g (1½ lb) spring greens

---

about 600 ml (1 pint) sunflower oil

7.5 ml (1½ level tsp) caster sugar

---

salt

---

25 g (1 oz) natural roasted peanuts, halved

---

1 Discard the thick stems from the spring greens and wash the leaves. Dry thoroughly, then roll the leaves together tightly, a few at a time, and shred them very finely with a sharp knife. Spread out on absorbent kitchen paper and pat dry with more paper (the shreds must be completely dry before frying).

2 Heat the oil in a wok or large, deep frying pan until just smoking, then remove from the heat and add the spring greens. Stir well, return the pan to the heat and fry for about 2 minutes, stirring.

3 Using a slotted spoon, carefully remove the fried greens to a plate lined with absorbent kitchen paper and drain for a few moments.

4 Turn the greens on to a warm plate and sprinkle with the sugar, salt to taste and nuts.

VARIATION

Toast sunflower seeds and toss into steamed spring greens or your favourite green vegetable with garlic butter.

Quick Stir-fry

PREPARATION TIME: 15 MINUTES
COOKING TIME: 10-15 MINUTES
SERVES 6
225 CALORIES PER SERVING

25 ml (1 fl oz) oil
3 large bunches of spring onions, trimmed and sliced diagonally
350 g (12 oz) beansprouts
two 227 g (8 oz) cans of water chestnuts, drained and sliced horizontally
2-3 large red peppers, about 550 g (1¼ lb) total weight, deseeded and sliced into matchsticks
550 g (1¼ lb) red cabbage, finely shredded
200 ml (7 fl oz) rice or distilled malt vinegar
15-30 ml (1-2 level tbsp) chilli sauce (see Cook's Tip)
125 g (4 oz) caster sugar
salt and pepper

1 Heat the oil in a wok until smoking, then stir-fry the spring onions, beansprouts and water chestnuts for 2-3 minutes over a high heat. Remove from the pan and set aside.

2 Add the peppers and cabbage to the pan and stir-fry for 2-3 minutes. Stir in the vinegar, chilli sauce and sugar. Season with salt and pepper. Stir-fry over a high heat for 5-10 minutes.

3 Return the spring onion mixture to the wok. Toss over a high heat for 1 minute. Season and serve.

COOK'S TIP

Some chilli sauces are hotter than others, so add to taste. You can stir in extra at the end for a hotter dish.

Asparagus and Mangetout with Chinese Lemon Sauce

PREPARATION TIME: 10 MINUTES
COOKING TIME: 10 MINUTES
SERVES 4
130 CALORIES PER SERVING

225 g (8 oz) asparagus spears

salt

15 ml (1 tbsp) vegetable oil

5 ml (1 tsp) sesame oil

225 g (8 oz) mangetout, topped and tailed

1 garlic clove, skinned and crushed

30 ml (2 tbsp) dry sherry

15 ml (1 level tbsp) caster sugar

10 ml (2 tsp) light soy sauce

grated rind and juice of 1 lemon

5 ml (1 level tsp) cornflour

15 ml (1 level tbsp) toasted sesame seeds, for sprinkling

strips of lemon rind and coriander sprigs, to garnish

1 Cut off the woody part of the asparagus stems and cut the asparagus diagonally into three or four pieces. Cook in boiling salted water for about 5 minutes or until just tender. Drain well.

2 Heat the oils in a wok or frying pan and fry the mangetout, garlic and asparagus for 2 minutes.

3 In a bowl, mix the sherry with the sugar, soy sauce, lemon rind and juice, cornflour and 75 ml (5 tbsp) water.

4 Stir the mixture into the pan and cook until the sauce thickens and coats the vegetables. Sprinkle with the sesame seeds and garnish with lemon rind and coriander sprigs.

Creamy Green Beans

PREPARATION TIME: 10 MINUTES
COOKING TIME: 4 MINUTES
SERVES 8
60 CALORIES PER SERVING

700 g (1½ lb) fine green beans, topped and tailed

salt and pepper

30 ml (2 level tbsp) mayonnaise

30 ml (2 level tbsp) natural yogurt

15 ml (1 level tbsp) wholegrain mustard

1 Cook the beans in boiling salted water for about 4 minutes. Drain well.

2 Mix together the remaining ingredients, season with salt and pepper, and stir in the hot beans. Serve hot.

VARIATION

Leave the beans to cool before mixing with the mayonnaise, yogurt and mustard. Serve cold as a salad.

Spicy Potatoes

PREPARATION TIME: 5 MINUTES
COOKING TIME: 25 MINUTES
SERVES 4-6
210-140 CALORIES PER SERVING

---

700 g (1½ lb) waxy potatoes, scrubbed

---

salt and pepper

---

30 ml (2 tbsp) olive oil

---

2 garlic cloves, skinned and chopped

---

1 green chilli, deseeded and chopped

---

5 ml (1 level tsp) mild paprika

---

400 g (14 oz) can of chopped tomatoes

---

chopped fresh parsley, to garnish

---

1 Cook the potatoes in boiling salted water until just tender. Drain and leave to cool.

2 Meanwhile, heat the oil in a deep frying pan, add the garlic, chilli and paprika, and fry gently for 2 minutes, stirring all the time. Add the tomatoes, increase the heat and simmer for about 10 minutes or until the sauce is reduced and very thick.

3 Carefully peel the potatoes, and cut into large chunks. Add to the tomato sauce and cook for about 10 minutes, stirring occasionally, until the sauce is reduced further and just clings to the potato. Season with salt and pepper. Serve warm or cold, sprinkled generously with parsley.

Lemon-glazed Vegetables

PREPARATION TIME: 15 MINUTES
COOKING TIME: 18 MINUTES
SERVES 4
105 CALORIES PER SERVING

225 g (8 oz) baby carrots

225 g (8 oz) turnip, trimmed and cut into lengths

4 celery sticks, trimmed and cut in three on the diagonal

300 ml (½ pint) water

grated rind and juice of 1 lemon

sprig of fresh chervil

25 ml (1½ level tbsp) sugar

25 g (1 oz) butter

salt and pepper

4 small courgettes, cut into lengths

30 ml (2 level tbsp) chopped fresh chervil, to garnish

1 Place the carrots, turnips and celery in a heavy-based saucepan and pour the water over. Add the lemon rind and juice, chervil sprig, sugar and butter, and season with salt and pepper.

2 Lay a buttered piece of greaseproof paper on top of the vegetables, bring to the boil and simmer for 10 minutes. Add the courgettes and cook, uncovered, for about 5 minutes, turning occasionally, until tender. Using a slotted spoon, remove the vegetables and keep warm. Boil the sauce for 3 minutes until thickened to a lemony glaze, then pour over the vegetables. Garnish with the chervil and serve.

Raw Vegetables with Garlic Dressing

PREPARATION TIME: 20 MINUTES
SERVES 4
250 CALORIES PER SERVING

175 g (6 oz) carrots, peeled

175 g (6 oz) courgettes

175 g (6 oz) celeriac

15 ml (1 tbsp) lemon juice

175 g (6 oz) raw beetroot, peeled

90 ml (6 tbsp) olive or vegetable oil

30 ml (2 tbsp) wine vinegar

2.5 ml (½ level tsp) sugar

2.5 ml (½ level tsp) mustard powder

1 garlic clove, skinned and crushed

salt and pepper

chopped fresh parsley, to garnish

1 Grate the carrots and courgettes into a bowl.

2 Peel and grate the celeriac, toss immediately in the lemon juice and add to the carrot and courgette mixture. Lastly, grate the beetroot and add to the mixture.

3 Put the oil, vinegar, sugar, mustard and garlic in a screw-topped jar and season with salt and pepper. Shake the jar until the dressing is thoroughly combined.

4 Pour the dressing over the vegetables and toss lightly just to coat. Serve immediately, garnished with chopped parsley.

Parsnips in a Lime Glaze

PREPARATION TIME: 5 MIN·UTES
COOKING TIME: 15 MINUTES
SERVES 4
225 CALORIES PER SERVING

700 g (1½ lb) parsnips

salt and pepper

1 lime

50 g (2 oz) butter

25 g (1 oz) light muscovado sugar

thyme sprigs, to garnish

1 Peel the parsnips and trim off the tops and roots. Cut in half lengthways. (If using older, tougher parsnips, cut into quarters and remove the woody cores.) Add to a pan of boiling salted water and cook for 5 minutes.

2 Meanwhile, using a canelle knife or vegetable peeler, carefully pare thin slivers of rind from the lime; set aside for the garnish. Halve the lime and squeeze out the juice.

3 Melt the butter in a large saucepan together with the sugar. Add the lime juice and heat gently, stirring, to dissolve the sugar.

4 Drain the parsnips thoroughly in a colander, then add to the lime mixture in the saucepan. Toss in the buttery lime mixture and cook over a moderate heat, shaking the pan frequently, for about 10 minutes or until golden brown.

5 Transfer to a warmed serving dish and garnish with the slivers of lime zest and thyme sprigs.

VARIATIONS

Replace 1 parsnip with 3 eddoes. Peel and halve the eddoes and cook with the parsnips. Alternatively use carrots or turnips instead of parsnips. A handful of walnuts tossed in towards the end of the cooking time adds a delicious crunch.

Swede and Carrot Gratin

PREPARATION TIME: 10 MINUTES
COOKING TIME: 20 MINUTES
SERVES 6
420 CALORIES PER SERVING

butter

50 g (2 oz) fresh brown breadcrumbs

50 g (2 oz) medium oatmeal

75 g (3 oz) mature Cheddar cheese, coarsely grated

15 ml (1 level tbsp) chopped fresh parsley

salt and pepper

700 g (1½ lb) swede, peeled and coarsely grated

450 g (1 lb) carrots, peeled and coarsely grated

45 ml (3 tbsp) orange juice

142 ml (5 fl oz) carton of double cream

1 Melt 50 g (2 oz) butter in a large, shallow, flameproof casserole. Stir in the breadcrumbs and oatmeal, and fry gently for 2-3 minutes or until just beginning to crisp, then transfer to a bowl to cool. Stir in the cheese, parsley and plenty of salt and pepper.

2 Wipe out the casserole and melt a further 75 g (3 oz) butter. Add the swede and carrot, and cook for 7-10 minutes or until almost tender, stirring occasionally. Stir in the orange juice and cream, and season well.

3 Bring to a gentle simmer, cover and cook for about 5 minutes or until tender, stirring occasionally.

4 Sprinkle over the crumbs to cover and grill until golden brown.

Lemon Spinach

PREPARATION TIME: 10 MINUTES
COOKING TIME: 5 MINUTES
SERVES 6
100 CALORIES PER SERVING

900 g (2 lb) fresh young spinach
50 g (2 oz) butter
4 garlic cloves, skinned and crushed
45 ml (3 tbsp) lemon juice
salt and pepper
freshly grated nutmeg

1 Wash the spinach thoroughly and drain well. Discard any large stalks.

2 Melt the butter in a very large saucepan, add the garlic and sauté for 1 minute. Add the spinach and stir well until coated in the garlic butter.

3 Cover tightly and cook for about 2 minutes or until the spinach has just softened but is still bright green.

4 Lift out of the pan using draining spoons. Add the lemon juice and season with salt, pepper and nutmeg. Serve immediately.

Quick Vegetable Ideas

Add interest to your vegetable side dishes with the following suggestions:

✦ Grill rashers of streaky bacon until crisp, roughly chop and scatter over cooked Brussels sprouts with pared Parmesan cheese.

✦ Canned lima beans are excellent with grilled meats. Reheat with crushed garlic, a bay leaf and a knob of butter.

✦ Stir small cubes of blue brie into mashed potato, allowing the cheese to melt before serving.

✦ Spoon 30 ml (2 tbsp) of your favourite vinaigrette over 450 g (1 lb) cooked green vegetables.

✦ Melt 50 g (2 oz) butter in a frying pan. Add 50 g (2 oz) jumbo or rolled oats and 50 g (2 oz) chopped, mixed nuts, and fry until golden. Season well and scatter over cooked vegetables.

Mixed-leaf and Parmesan Salad

PREPARATION TIME: 10 MINUTES
SERVES 6
125 CALORIES PER SERVING

125 g (4 oz) young spinach leaves

125 g (4 oz) young rocket leaves

125 g (4 oz) flat-leaf parsley

Parmesan cheese

To serve

balsamic vinegar

olive oil

pepper

warm ciabatta

1 Wash and dry the spinach, rocket and parsley, and toss together in a salad bowl.

2 Use a vegetable peeler to pare off shavings of Parmesan, and scatter over the salad leaves.

3 Serve the salad, allowing each person to drizzle balsamic vinegar and oil over their salad. Season with pepper and serve warm ciabatta as an accompaniment.

COOK'S TIP

For an even quicker salad, buy a pack of ready-washed mixed salad leaves from the supermarket.

Crisp Vegetable Salad

PREPARATION TIME: 20 MINUTES
COOKING TIME: 5 MINUTES
SERVES 6
170 CALORIES PER SERVING

salt and pepper

450 g (1 lb) broccoli

225 g (8 oz) asparagus

150 g (5 oz) mangetout

450 g (1 lb) fennel

For the dressing

90 ml (6 tbsp) olive oil

30 ml (2 tbsp) white wine vinegar

5 ml (1 level tsp) Dijon mustard

salt and pepper

1 Put a large saucepan of salted water on to boil. Meanwhile, trim the broccoli into bite-sized florets. Cut the tips plus 2.5 cm (1 inch) of stalk off the asparagus. Top and tail the mangetout and cut the fennel into large chunks, reserving the feathery tops for the dressing.

2 When the water is bubbling furiously, plunge the asparagus and mangetout in for 1 minute. Meanwhile, fill a bowl with cold water and add some ice cubes.

3 Remove the asparagus and the mangetout from the pan with a slotted spoon and plunge into the cold water for 1 minute. Lift the vegetables out of the water and drain well.

4 Add the broccoli and fennel to the boiling water and simmer for 3 minutes. Transfer to the cold water and cool for 2-3 minutes. Drain well. Toss all the vegetables together in a bowl. Cover and chill.

5 Whisk all the dressing ingredients together with the finely chopped fennel tops. Season with salt and pepper.

6 About 30 minutes before serving the salad, gently toss the vegetables and dressing together. Serve at room temperature.

Tomato and Olive Salad

PREPARATION TIME: 15 MINUTES
SERVES 6
190 CALORIES PER SERVING

700 g (1½ lb) ripe tomatoes
75 g (3 oz) pitted black olives
1 shallot or small onion
90 ml (6 tbsp) olive oil
30 ml (2 tbsp) white wine vinegar
2.5 ml (½ level tsp) salt
10 ml (2 level tsp) Dijon mustard
pepper
75 ml (5 level tbsp) single cream
15 ml (1 level tbsp) chopped fresh parsley

1 Peel the tomatoes, if wished (see page 144). Quarter and deseed, then roughly chop them. Chop the olives and shallot, and whisk with the remaining ingredients.

2 Toss the tomatoes with the dressing and serve.

Mixed *L*eaf, Orange and Strawberry Salad

PREPARATION TIME: 20 MINUTES
SERVES 6
150 CALORIES PER SERVING

1 small frisée lettuce
1 bunch of watercress
3 large oranges
225 g (8 oz) strawberries
1 large ripe avocado
45 ml (3 tbsp) olive oil
5 ml (1 tsp) white wine vinegar
5 ml (1 tsp) Dijon mustard
salt and pepper

1 Wash and dry the frisée and watercress, removing any coarse or discoloured stalks or leaves. Tear into small pieces and place in a large serving bowl.

2 Peel the oranges and slice into the serving bowl. Wash, hull and slice the strawberries. Halve, peel and slice the avocado. Place both in the bowl.

3 To make the dressing, whisk together the olive oil, wine vinegar and Dijon mustard, and season with salt and pepper. Pour the dressing over the prepared salad, toss well and serve.

Tuna Bean Salad

PREPARATION TIME: 15 MINUTES
SERVES 4-6
805-540 CALORIES PER SERVING

150 ml (¼ pint) olive oil

60 ml (4 tbsp) lemon juice

2 garlic cloves, skinned and crushed

salt and pepper

two 425 g (15 oz) cans of cannellini beans, drained

2 small red onions, skinned

two 200 g (7 oz) cans of tuna fish in oil

chopped parsley, to garnish

1 Whisk together the oil, lemon juice, garlic and seasoning in a bowl. Add the beans and mix well.

2 Slice the onions very thinly and stir gently into the beans. Drain the tuna, reserving the oil. Coarsely flake the tuna and add to the beans with the reserved oil. Toss gently and adjust the seasoning. Stir gently and sprinkle liberally with parsley to serve.

Greek Salad

PREPARATION TIME: 15 MINUTES
SERVES 4-6
525-350 CALORIES PER SERVING

700 g (1½ lb) tomatoes
1 cucumber
1 large green pepper
225 g (8 oz) feta cheese
125 g (4 oz) black olives, pitted
For the dressing
135 ml (9 tbsp) olive oil
45 ml (3 tbsp) lemon juice
15 ml (1 level tbsp) chopped fresh oregano
large pinch of sugar
pepper

1 Slice the tomatoes and arrange in a serving bowl. Halve the cucumber length-ways, then slice. Halve and deseed the pepper, then cut into strips. Cut the feta cheese into dice.

2 Whisk the dressing ingredients together in a jug or shake together in a screw-topped jar.

3 Add the cucumber, green pepper, feta and olives to the salad bowl. Pour over the dressing and toss gently. Serve at once.

Salad Baskets

PREPARATION TIME: 15 MINUTES
COOKING TIME: 12 MINUTES
SERVES 6
225 CALORIES PER SERVING

---

6 slices of white sliced bread

---

50 ml (2 fl oz) olive oil

---

2 pickled dill cucumbers, plus 50 ml (2 fl oz) of the pickling vinegar

---

6 pieces of sun-dried tomatoes in oil plus 25 ml (1 fl oz) oil from the sun-dried tomatoes

---

9 anchovy fillets

---

75 g (3 oz) Mozzarella or Edam cheese

---

handful of small green salad leaves, preferably lamb's lettuce

---

flat-leaf parsley, to garnish

---

1 Remove the bread crusts and roll out the bread thinly with a rolling pin. Stamp or cut out a 9 cm (3½ inch) round from each slice. Brush one side lightly with a little of the oil. Press into deep bun tins and bake at 200°C (400°F) mark 6 for 10-12 minutes. Cool.

2 Blend the oil and pickling vinegar with two sun-dried tomatoes.

3 Chop the remaining sun-dried tomatoes. Halve the anchovy fillets. Finely chop the dill cucumbers. Dice the cheese. Fill each 'bread basket' with a mixture of salad leaves, tomatoes, cucumber and cheese. Spoon a little dressing over each basket to serve. Garnish with parsley.

COOK'S TIP

The baskets can be made 2-3 days ahead and stored in an airtight container. If you have no deep bun tins, use oiled ramekins.

Mediterranean Pasta Salad

PREPARATION TIME: 15 MINUTES + STANDING
COOKING TIME: 2-10 MINUTES
SERVES 4
415 CALORIES PER SERVING

The flavours of the Mediterranean are captured in this salad of pasta, sun-dried tomatoes, black olives, basil leaves, shredded spring onions and cherry tomatoes. Any pasta shapes can be used: if preferred use tricolore pasta - a mixture of spinach, tomato and plain pasta.

175 g (6 oz) fresh or dried pasta shapes

30 ml (2 tbsp) extra-virgin olive oil

4 sun-dried tomatoes in oil, drained

4-6 spring onions

225 g (8 oz) cherry tomatoes

8-12 basil leaves

about 8-12 black olives

For the dressing

2 sun-dried tomatoes in oil, drained

30 ml (2 tbsp) oil from the sun-dried tomato jar

30 ml (2 tbsp) red wine vinegar

1 garlic clove

15 ml (1 level tbsp) tomato purée

pinch of sugar (optional)

salt and pepper

30 ml (2 tbsp) extra-virgin olive oil

1 Cook the pasta in boiling salted water with 15 ml (1 tbsp) olive oil added until *al dente* (just tender but still firm to the bite). Fresh pasta will only take 2-3 minutes; for dried pasta refer to the packet instructions. Drain the pasta in a colander, then refresh under cold running water. Drain thoroughly and transfer to a large bowl. Stir in 15 ml (1 tbsp) olive oil to prevent the pasta sticking.

2 Slice the sun-dried tomatoes. Trim and finely shred the spring onions. Halve the cherry tomatoes. Tear the basil leaves into smaller pieces, if preferred.

3 Add the sun-dried and cherry tomatoes, spring onions, olives and basil to the pasta and toss to mix.

4 To make the dressing, put the sun-dried tomatoes (with their oil), vinegar, garlic and tomato purée in a blender or food processor. Add the sugar, if using, and salt and pepper. With the motor running, pour the oil through the feeder tube, and process briefly to make a fairly thick dressing.

5 Pour the dressing over the pasta and toss well. If possible, cover and leave to stand to allow the flavours to mingle for 1-2 hours before serving.

COOK'S TIP
Take extra care to avoid overcooking the pasta and quickly cool it under cold running water to preserve the texture.

VARIATION
Toss cubes of mature vegetarian Cheddar into the salad and serve with wholemeal bread and a leafy green salad for a main course.

Warm Seafood Salad with Toasted Polenta

PREPARATION TIME: 15 MINUTES
COOKING TIME: 15 MINUTES
SERVES 6
210 CALORIES PER SERVING

75 g (3 oz) polenta (see Note)

150 ml (5 fl oz) low-calorie salad dressing

1 garlic clove, skinned and crushed

30 ml (2 level tbsp) chopped fresh herbs, such as thyme, chives, parsley

350 g (12 oz) smoked haddock fillet

175 g (6 oz) cooked peeled prawns

1 Make up the polenta according to packet instructions. Spoon on to a sheet of foil, cool slightly, then press into a rectangle about 1 cm (½ inch) thick. Cool.

2 Whisk together the dressing, garlic and half of the herbs. Thinly slice the haddock. Place the fish and prawns in a single layer in a shallow, heatproof dish. Pour the dressing over. Cover and chill.

3 Cut the cooled polenta in 7.5 cm (3 inch) triangles. Grill for about 4 minutes on each side or until golden.

4 Grill the fish for 1-2 minutes, basting, until the haddock turns opaque. Serve the polenta with the warm salad. Sprinkle the remaining herbs over.

NOTE

Polenta is coarse-grained, yellow cornmeal which is cooked in water to a thick paste. The quick-cook variety is suitable for this recipe. Look for it in supermarkets and Italian delicatessens.

Spinach, Bacon and Roquefort Salad

PREPARATION TIME: 15 MINUTES
COOKING TIME: 10 MINUTES
SERVES 8
520 CALORIES PER SERVING.

8 slices of French bread, cut on the diagonal, about 2.5 cm (1 inch) thick

120 ml (8 tbsp) olive oil

175 g (6 oz) streaky bacon or pancetta, sliced very thinly

50 g (2 oz) pine nuts

125 g (4 oz) Roquefort cheese

175 g (6 oz) black seedless grapes

125 g (4 oz) young spinach leaves

60 ml (4 tbsp) sesame oil

30 ml (2 tbsp) red wine vinegar

pepper

1 Brush both sides of each slice of French bread with 60 ml (4 tbsp) of the olive oil. Place on a baking sheet. Halve or chop the bacon and place on a baking sheet with the pine nuts. Place the baking sheets in the oven and cook at 230°C (450°F) mark 8 for about 10 minutes or until golden brown, turning halfway through.

2 Crumble the Roquefort, halve the grapes, wash the spinach. Whisk the remaining 60 ml (4 tbsp) olive oil with the sesame oil, vinegar and pepper.

3 Pile the spinach, bacon, cheese, pine nuts and grapes on the croûtes and serve.

Quick Salad Ideas

*To cheer up a basic mixture of green salad leaves, toss in
one of the following, depending on what else in in the fridge
or storecupboard:*

◆ Plenty of crispy fried or grilled, snipped bacon with the warm bacon fat, chopped chives and a drop of vinegar, to dress the leaves.

◆ Coarsely grated cheese – Gruyère or Emmental are ideal. Cheese with vinaigrette is a delicious combination.

◆ Fry a sliced onion and a sliced apple together in a little olive oil until crisp and golden. Off the heat, add one or two spoonfuls of vinaigrette and some apple juice and toss it all into the leaves.

◆ Peel and slice an orange. Snip one or two spring onions. Roughly chop some roast peanuts or cashews. Add to the salad with vinaigrette. Sliced strawberries are also delicious tossed in.

◆ When you're making up your dressing, whisk in a spoonful of cream. It could be single or double or even crème fraîche with a little wholegrain mustard. This is particularly good with grilled pork.

◆ Pan-fry some chopped spring onions in olive oil with a little grated fresh root ginger. Off the heat, add the juice of an orange and a dash of bottled Teriyaki marinade. Toss and serve immediately.

Desserts

Lemon and Raspberry Puffs

PREPARATION TIME: 15 MINUTES
COOKING TIME: 15 MINUTES
SERVES 6
120 CALORIES PER SERVING

You can use either fresh or frozen raspberries to prepare these soufflés.

very low-fat spread
225 g (8 oz) raspberries
15 g (½ oz) icing sugar
25 g (1 oz) plain flour
200 ml (7 fl oz) skimmed milk
2 eggs
25 g (1 oz) caster sugar
finely grated rind and juice of 2 lemons
icing sugar, to dust

1 Lightly grease six 150 ml (¼ pint) ramekin dishes.

2 Purée the raspberries and icing sugar in a food processor. Rub through a nylon sieve to remove the pips, then divide the purée among the ramekin dishes.

3 Melt 40 g (1½ oz) low-fat spread in a medium-sized saucepan. Add the flour, then gradually blend in the milk. Bring to the boil, stirring, and cook for about 1 minute, whisking the mixture until smooth. Cool slightly.

4 Beat in the egg yolks, followed by the caster sugar, the finely grated rind of the lemons and 45 ml (3 tbsp) lemon juice.

5 Whisk the egg whites until stiff but not dry. Using a large, metal spoon, beat one small spoonful of egg white into the sauce to lighten it, then carefully fold in the remainder. Spoon the mixture into the prepared dishes and place on a baking sheet.

6 Bake in the oven at 190°C (375°F) mark 5 for 15-20 minutes or until lightly set. Dust with icing sugar and serve immediately.

Clementines in Brandy

PREPARATION TIME: 10-15 MINUTES
SERVES 6
140 CALORIES PER SERVING

10 clementines or other seedless 'easy peelers'

12 pitted dates or no-soak prunes

juice of 1 lemon

30 ml (2 level tbsp) caster sugar

60 ml (4 tbsp) brandy

1 Peel the clementines. Remove as much pith as possible, then thickly slice the fruit into a bowl. Roughly slice the dates or prunes and stir into the clementines.

2 Stir the lemon juice, sugar and brandy into the fruit. Cover and chill until required.

Hot Raspberry and Mascarpone Brûlée

PREPARATION TIME: **10** MINUTES
COOKING TIME: **5** MINUTES
SERVES **6**
270 CALORIES PER SERVING

*For a deliciously different pudding try this quick brûlée.
Make up to the end of step 1 a few hours ahead and chill if
necessary. It is then ready to grill and serve in minutes.*

---

350 g (12 oz) fresh raspberries

---

250 g (9 oz) mascarpone cheese or low-fat soft cheese,
softened with a little single cream

---

125 g (4 oz) caster sugar

---

1 Put the raspberries in a large heatproof dish or divide them among six
individual gratin dishes or ramekins. Dot with spoonfuls of mascarpone.

2 Sprinkle with the caster sugar. Place under a very hot, preheated grill for 2-3
minutes or until the sugar has caramelised and the fruit is just bubbling. Serve
warm.

VARIATION

Replace the raspberries with 350 g (12 oz) halved, stoned and sliced fresh apricots. Mix them with 30 ml (2 level tbsp) toasted flaked almonds. If the apricots
are very tart, toss them in a little extra sugar. Complete as above.

Hot Mango and Banana Salad

PREPARATION TIME: 10 MINUTES
COOKING TIME: 5 MINUTES
SERVES 4
200 CALORIES PER SERVING

2 large oranges
2 firm but ripe mangoes, about 700 g (1½ lb) total weight
4 small bananas
25 g (1 oz) very low-fat spread
light soft brown sugar
30 ml (2 tbsp) Malibu or rum
30 ml (2 tbsp) lemon or lime juice

1 Coarsely grate the rind and squeeze the juice of one orange. Peel the other one with a serrated knife and slice thickly. Peel the mangoes with a vegetable peeler. Slice the mango flesh either side of the central stone. Remove any flesh from around the stone and cut all the flesh into bite-sized pieces. Peel and thickly slice the bananas.

2 Melt the low-fat spread in a large, non-stick frying pan. Add 5 ml (1 level tsp) sugar with the mango and banana, and sauté for about 2-3 minutes or until just beginning to soften.

3 Pour in the Malibu or rum, all of the fruit juice and the orange slices. Bring to the boil, then serve immediately, decorated with the grated orange rind.

Glazed Nectarine Tart

PREPARATION TIME: 10 MINUTES
COOKING TIME: 15 MINUTES
SERVES 6
165 CALORIES PER SERVING

175 g (6 oz) puff pastry

550 g (1¼ lb) ripe nectarines or peaches

25 g (1 oz) very low-fat spread, melted

30 ml (2 level tbsp) apricot jam

1 Thinly roll out the pastry to a 28 cm (11 inch) round. Place on a non-stick baking sheet and prick well all over. Bake in the oven at 230°C (450°F) mark 8 for 8-10 minutes or until well browned and cooked through.

2 Meanwhile, quarter, stone and roughly slice the nectarines or peaches.

3 Brush melted spread over the pastry and scatter the fruit over, right to the edges of the pastry. Drizzle with the remaining spread and grill for 5 minutes or until the fruit is just tinged with colour. Cool slightly.

4 Warm the apricot jam with a little water and brush over the fruit to glaze. Serve warm.

VARIATION

Bake the pastry base for 6-7 minutes only or until golden. Top with 75 g (3 oz) marzipan rolled out to as thin a round as possible. Return to the oven for about 2 minutes or until the marzipan begins to melt. Top with peaches as above. Grill for 3-4 minutes and serve immediately without glazing. Serve with a little low-fat fromage frais if wished.

Cinnamon-toasted Malt Loaf

PREPARATION TIME: 10 MINUTES
COOKING TIME: 3-4 MINUTES
SERVES 6
190 CALORIES PER SERVING

1 malt loaf, about 225 g (8 oz)

25 g (1 oz) low-fat spread

1.25 ml (¼ level tsp) ground cinnamon

30 ml (2 level tbsp) demerara sugar

2 ripe pears

6 scoops of frozen yogurt

ground cinnamon for dusting (optional)

1 Slice the malt loaf into about 12 slices. Mix the low-fat spread with the cinnamon.

2 Spread each slice of the malt loaf with a little of the cinnamon mixture. Sprinkle with the demerara sugar. Place the slices of malt loaf, spread-side up, on a baking sheet. Grill on that side only for 3-4 minutes or until they are hot. Meanwhile, peel, core and thinly slice the pears.

3 Place two slices of malt loaf in each bowl and serve with a scoop of frozen yogurt and some slices of pear. Dust with a little ground cinnamon, if wished. Serve immediately.

Roasted Peaches with Pistachio Stuffing

PREPARATION TIME: 15 MINUTES
COOKING TIME: 20 MINUTES
SERVES 6
175 CALORIES PER SERVING

50 g (2 oz) amaretti biscuits

75 g (3 oz) shelled pistachio nuts

25 g (1 oz) light muscovado sugar

1.25 ml (¼ level tsp) Chinese five-spice powder

2 egg yolks

6 peaches (see Cook's Tip)

Greek-style yogurt or crème fraîche, to serve

1 Roughly crush the amaretti biscuits between two sheets of greaseproof paper, using a rolling pin; or by processing briefly in a food processor. Finely chop the pistachios. Mix the crushed biscuits and pistachios in a bowl with the sugar, spice and egg yolks.

2 Cut the peaches in half and remove the stones. Pile the nut filling into the peach halves and place them in a baking dish. Pour 150 ml (¼ pint) water around the peaches and bake in the oven at 180°C (350°F) mark 4 for 20 minutes or until the peaches are soft.

3 Transfer the stuffed peaches to individual serving plates and serve immediately, accompanied by Greek yogurt or crème fraîche.

COOK'S TIP

The cooking time depends very much on the ripeness of the peaches. If you have a choice, select fruits that are almost, but not quite, ripe enough to eat.

Instead of Greek yogurt, serve the peaches with a sabayon sauce. To make this, put 2 egg yolks, 25 g (1 oz) caster sugar and 60 ml (4 tbsp) medium dry white wine in a large bowl over a pan of barely simmering water. Whisk using an electric beater or large balloon whisk for about 10 minutes until the mixture is creamy and frothy.

Caramelised Pineapple

PREPARATION TIME: 10 MINUTES + CHILLING
COOKING TIME: 10 MINUTES
SERVES 6
140 CALORIES PER SERVING

125 g (4 oz) caster sugar
250 ml (9 fl oz) white wine
25 g (1 oz) soft brown sugar
2.5 cm (1 inch) piece of fresh root ginger, peeled and thinly sliced
6 thin slices of fresh pineapple

1 In a heavy-based saucepan, melt the caster sugar over a very low heat until pale golden and liquid.

2 Off the heat, add the wine (it will splutter), soft brown sugar and ginger. Simmer, stirring, until reduced by about a third. Strain over the pineapple slices and cool. Cover and chill before serving.

Rhubarb and Apple Crisp

PREPARATION TIME: 15 MINUTES
COOKING TIME: 5 MINUTES
SERVES 6
140 CALORIES PER SERVING

450 g (1 lb) rhubarb
2 eating apples
100 ml (4 fl oz) unsweetened orange juice
5 ml (1 level tsp) ground cinnamon
demerara sugar
125 g (4 oz) wholemeal breadcrumbs
15 g (½ oz) very low-fat spread, melted

1 Chop the rhubarb into 2.5 cm (1 inch) pieces. Peel, quarter, core and slice the apples and place in a saucepan with the rhubarb, orange juice, cinnamon and 25 g (1 oz) sugar. Cover and gently poach for about 5 minutes or until the rhubarb is just tender.

2 Meanwhile, mix the breadcrumbs and melted low-fat spread with 25 g (1 oz) sugar. Toast under the grill until lightly browned.

3 Divide half the crumb mixture among six individual dishes, cover with the fruit and top with the remaining breadcrumbs. Serve warm or cold.

Cranberry and Raspberry Mousse

PREPARATION TIME: 10 MINUTES
COOKING TIME: 5 MINUTES
SERVES 6
40 CALORIES PER SERVING

25 g (1 oz) pitted dates
225 g (8 oz) each fresh or frozen cranberries and raspberries
2.5 ml (½ level tsp) arrowroot
15 ml (1 tbsp) orange juice
15 ml (1 level tbsp) honey
200 ml (7 fl oz) chilled skimmed milk
2.5 ml (½ tsp) vanilla essence
fresh berries, to decorate

1 Roughly chop the dates and place in a saucepan with the cranberries, raspberries and 15 ml (1 tbsp) water. Blend the arrowroot with the orange juice. Stir into the fruit and bring to the boil. Simmer for 4-5 minutes, stirring, until the fruit is very soft and the mixture lightly thickened. Cool slightly, then sieve. Mix in the honey and chill.

2 Divide half the fruit purée among six glasses. Place the chilled skimmed milk and vanilla essence in a food processor. Process for 2-3 minutes or until the consistency is like whipped cream. Fold the remaining fruit purée into the cream and spoon into the glasses. Decorate to serve.

Cheat's Summer Brûlée

PREPARATION TIME: 20 MINUTES
COOKING TIME: 10 MINUTES
SERVES 6
400 CALORIES PER SERVING

This impressive pudding is surprisingly easy to make. A little
Cointreau could be mixed with the fruit.

225 g (8 oz) strawberries
2 ripe peaches
2 bananas
30 ml (2 tbsp) lemon juice
284 ml (10 fl oz) carton of double cream
142 ml (5 fl oz) Greek natural yogurt
175 g (6 oz) caster sugar

1 Hull and halve the strawberries. Slice the peaches. Slice the bananas and toss in the lemon juice. Mix the fruit together then divide half of it among six small dishes.

2 Whip the cream until it forms soft peaks. Stir in the yogurt with the remaining fruit. Divide among the dishes, cover and chill until required.

3 Place the sugar in a small, heavy-based pan and just cover with cold water. Over a low heat, let all the sugar dissolve, without stirring.

4 When the liquid is clear, increase the heat and bubble furiously until it turns a light caramel brown.

5 Off the heat, let the caramel cool until the bubbles subside and it starts to thicken. Pour in zigzags over the cream. Allow to harden, then serve.

Pears Poached in Three Wines

PREPARATION TIME: 5 MINUTES
COOKING TIME: 25 MINUTES
SERVES 4
150 CALORIES PER SERVING

---

175 g (6 oz) sugar

---

350 ml (12 fl oz) water

---

150 ml (¼ pint) each red, white and rosé wine

---

1 cinnamon stick

---

1 strip each orange and lemon rind

---

2 bay leaves

---

6 ripe William or Packham pears, peeled, halved and cored

---

bay leaves, to decorate

---

1 Divide the sugar among three saucepans and add 100 ml (4 fl oz) water to each. Pour the red wine into one with the cinnamon stick; the rosé in the second with the orange and lemon rind and the bay leaves and white wine in the third.

2 Place the pans over a low heat and stir each to dissolve the sugar, then bring each to the boil and boil for 2 minutes. Add four pear halves to each pan, cover and simmer gently for 10-15 minutes or until just tender.

3 Remove the pears from the pans and transfer to a serving dish. Strain the syrups into one pan and boil hard for 3-5 minutes or until syrupy. Finely shred the orange and lemon rind. Add to the syrup, then pour over the pears and leave to cool. Serve decorated with bay leaves.

COOK'S TIP

Using three different types of wine gives the dish a very attractive look, but if preferred you can always use just one type of wine.

Grilled Fruit with Sweet Ginger Butter

PREPARATION TIME: 10 MINUTES
COOKING TIME: 5-7 MINUTES
SERVES 6
200 CALORIES PER SERVING

---

1 large mango

---

selection of tropical fruit (see Cook's Tips)

---

125 g (4 oz) unsalted butter

---

30 ml (2 level tbsp) finely chopped stem ginger or peeled, fresh root ginger

---

10 ml (2 level tsp) icing sugar

---

10 ml (2 tsp) lemon juice

---

natural yogurt or single cream, to serve

---

banana leaves, to decorate (optional)

---

1 Prepare the fruit. Melt the butter and stir in the ginger, sugar and lemon juice.

2 Place the fruit under a hot grill. Brush with the butter mixture and cook, turning and brushing with butter, for 5-7 minutes or until beginning to caramelise. Serve with yogurt or cream.

COOK'S TIPS

To prepare the mango, cut thick slices from each side of the stone. Score the flesh in a wide criss-cross pattern, then push the skin up towards the flesh to expose the mango chunks.

For the tropical fruit, use pineapple wedges, slices of pawpaw and banana halves.

Blackberry and Pear Cobbler

PREPARATION TIME: 5 MINUTES
COOKING TIME: 30 MINUTES
SERVES 4
405 CALORIES PER SERVING

450 g (1 lb) blackberries, washed

450 g (1 lb) ripe pears, such as Conference, peeled, cored
and thickly sliced

finely grated rind and juice of 1 lemon

2.5 ml (½ level tsp) ground cinnamon

For the topping

225 g (8 oz) self-raising flour

pinch of salt

50 g (2 oz) butter or margarine, well chilled and diced

25 g (1 oz) caster sugar

about 150 ml (¼ pint) milk, plus extra to glaze

1 Put the blackberries and pears into a saucepan with the lemon rind and juice, and the cinnamon. Simmer for 15-20 minutes or until the fruit is just tender. Remove from the heat and leave to cool.

2 To make the topping, place the flour and salt in a bowl. Rub in the butter until the mixture resembles fine crumbs. Stir in the sugar. Gradually add enough milk to make a fairly soft dough.

3 Roll out the dough on a lightly floured work surface until 1 cm (½ inch) thick. Cut out rounds using a fluted 5 cm (2 inch) pastry cutter.

4 Put the fruit in a pie dish and top with overlapping pastry rounds, leaving a gap in the centre. Brush the top of the pastry rounds with milk. Bake in the oven at 220°C (425°F) mark 7 for 10-15 minutes or until the pastry is golden brown. Serve hot.

Zabaglione

PREPARATION TIME: 25 MINUTES
SERVES 6
115 CALORIES PER SERVING

Zabaglione (zabaione) is one of the most well-known of Italian puddings. In the 17th century, a royal chef from Piedmont in the north-west is said to have accidentally spilled fortified wine into some custard, but many cooks from Veneto, including those from the world-famous Harry's Bar, would argue that this light, delicate pudding is theirs.

---

4 egg yolks

---

75 g (3 oz) caster sugar

---

120 ml (8 tbsp) Marsala or other dessert wine

---

1 Put the egg yolks and sugar in a large heatproof bowl (see Cook's Tip). Over a saucepan of barely simmering water, beat the egg yolks with the sugar until pale and thick, using an electric whisk. This will take at least 5 minutes.

2 Keep the whisk running and, tablespoon by tablespoon, gradually add the Marsala until the mixture is very thick and frothy and forms soft mounds. This will take at least 20 minutes, but it is vital that the wine is added slowly and the mixture thickens. If not, the mixture will separate. Pour into six glasses and immediately serve to your guests.

COOK'S TIP

Be sure to use a large bowl, as the mixture increases in volume as you whisk.

Fast Fruit Puddings

*Hot or cold, a fruit dessert is the ideal finish to a meal. The
following ideas are quick and easy to prepare.*

✦ Remove the zest and squeeze the juice of four limes. Heat 150 ml (¼ pint)
lime juice in a small saucepan with 45 ml (3 level tbsp) caster sugar. Bring to
the boil and allow to bubble for 2-3 minutes or until all the sugar has dissolved. Remove the peel and slice the flesh of a selection of tropical fruits,
such as papaya, melon or mango. Just before serving, add the lime zest to the
warm syrup. Arrange the fruits on serving plates and spoon over the lime
syrup. Serve immediately.

✦ Cook some chopped rhubarb with one crushed cardamom pod and a little
water until the rhubarb softens. Stir in enough sugar to taste (it should still
be quite tart). Simmer for a further 2-3 minutes, then push through a sieve.
Serve warm over scoops of vanilla, brown bread or stem ginger ice cream.

✦ Arrange a plate of raspberries or red loganberries and sliced, peeled peaches.
Finely chop a piece of stem ginger and mix into crème fraîche or fromage frais
with a little of the ginger syrup. Spoon on to the fruits and decorate with
mint sprigs.

✦ Scatter fresh raspberries evenly over a baking sheet, sprinkle with a little caster sugar and place in a warm oven for about 5 minutes only. To make it extra
special, sprinkle the raspberries with vanilla sugar and serve with spoonfuls of
thick clotted cream.

✦ Place 900 g (2 lb) Victoria plums (stoned) in a buttered, heatproof dish,
sprinkle with 75 g (3 oz) demerara sugar and then pour over 200 ml (7 fl oz)
port. Cook at 200°C (400°F) mark 6 for 20 minutes or until the plums are
tender. Serve warm or chilled with ice cream.

◆ Serve strawberries in a warm orange and cardamom syrup. Gently warm 300 ml (½ pint) orange juice with 15 ml (1 tbsp) honey and the crushed seeds of a cardamom pod. Hull and halve 450 g (1 lb) strawberries, add to the warm syrup and serve with vanilla ice cream.

◆ Marinate 450 g (1 lb) halved strawberries and segments of two oranges in 30 ml (2 tbsp) Cointreau for 20 minutes. Serve with crème fraîche.

◆ Sauté berries in melted butter for 30 seconds; serve immediately with a dash of balsamic vinegar and sugar to taste.

Fast Finishers

When time is short it's tempting not to bother with dessert,
but the following are quick ways to finish a meal in style.

◆ Buy crisp biscotti biscuits from an Italian delicatessen and arrange on a plate with a dollop of chilled mascarpone. Dust with cocoa powder or icing sugar and serve with a glass of *vin santo*. Dip the biscuits in the wine and then into the mascarpone – great for midweek dinner parties.

◆ Warm, fresh-from-the-oven cookies are a treat after supper with coffee. Simply beat together 75 g (3 oz) softened butter, granulated sugar and soft brown sugar. Add a beaten egg, a splash of vanilla essence and 175 g (6 oz) self-raising flour. Fold in the same quantity of chocolate drops. Shape into balls and bake at 180°C (350°F) mark 4 for 10 minutes or until golden.

◆ To make irresistible Chocolate Heaven, mix 225 g (8 oz) chopped plain chocolate, 30 ml (2 tbsp) of your favourite liqueur and 40 ml (3½ tbsp) golden syrup in a heatproof bowl. Melt in the microwave or over a pan of simmering water. Cool slightly. Whip 300 ml (½ pint) double cream until it *just* holds its shape. Fold into the chocolate mixture. Pour into small glasses and chill for as long as you can. Dust with cocoa powder before serving.

INDEX